Risen Sons
Flannery O'Connor's Vision of History

Risen Sons

Flannery O'Connor's Vision of History

John F. Desmond

The University of Georgia Press
Athens and London

Set in Linotron 202 Garamond 3
The paper in this book meets the guidelines for
permanence and durability of the Committee on
Production Guidelines for Book Longevity of the
Council on Library Resources.

Printed in the United States of America
91 90 89 88 87   5 4 3 2 1

Library of Congress Cataloging in Publication Data
Desmond, John F.
    Risen sons.
    Bibliography: p.
    Includes index.
    1. O'Connor, Flannery—Knowledge—History.
2. History in literature. I. Title.
PS3565.C57Z643   1987   813'.54   86-30828
ISBN 0-8203-0945-1 (alk. paper)

British Library Cataloging in Publication Data available.

Illustration on p. x is taken from *The Collected Works
of St. John of the Cross,* trans. Kieran Kavanaugh and
Otilio Rodriguez (Washington, D.C.: ICS Publications,
Institute of Carmelite Studies, 1979).

For Linda, Matthew, and Monica

Contents

Acknowledgments

The lines of influence that shape a critical study are as mysterious and invisible as those which shape the work of art itself. A brief remark made by one of my teachers, a Jesuit theologian, nearly three decades ago has as much to do with the genesis of this study as anything else. Nevertheless, more tangible debts of gratitude can and must be acknowledged: to teachers Victor A. Elconin, Calvin G. Thayer, R. R. Male, and Alphonse J. Fritz, who were there at the beginning to nurture my work. More recently, John R. May and Lewis P. Simpson have not only encouraged and deeply influenced my study but have also generously offered their time and the facilities of Louisiana State University to further my research. Sally Fitzgerald and Marion Montgomery contributed valuable critical insights at a crucial stage in the project, in addition to their continuing strong support. Closer to home, colleagues Louise Westling of the University of Oregon and Patrick Henry of Whitman College have been particularly helpful by sharing their mutual scholarly interests with me for several years, interests which have left their salutary mark on this study.

I am also indebted to the National Endowment for the Humanities for a grant to support research in the Ina Dillard Russell Library at Georgia College, Milledgeville, and to the library staff for their kind assistance with the O'Connor collection. Whitman College and Dean Edward E. Foster have been especially generous in allowing me time and resources to complete this study. Editors Charles East and Karen Orchard of the University of Georgia Press extended themselves graciously and helpfully in support of this project. Finally, I am very grateful to Roberta Skiles, whose skill and patience in preparing the manuscript have been truly extraordinary.

Chapter 5 of this study originally appeared in a somewhat different form in *Modern Age* (Summer/Fall 1983) under the title: "Flannery O'Connor and the History Behind the History." Chapter 6 originally appeared in *Thought* (December 1984) under the title: "Risen Sons: History, Consciousness, and Personality in the Fiction of Flannery O'Connor." I wish to thank the editors for permission to republish this material.

Introduction

In a reliquary at the Convent of the Incarnation in Avila, there is a small drawing in pen and ink of Christ on the cross. The drawing, given as a gift to one of the nuns at the convent, was done by the sixteenth-century mystic St. John of the Cross and represents a vision he had recently had. The sketch presents a remarkable and stunning visual perspective—the viewer looks down on the crucified Christ from an angle above and to the right of the cross, instead of the more conventional frontal view. The effect is revolutionary. The crucifix appears in one sense to be horizontal and in another, vertical. More important, the nailed figure of Christ on the cross appears in one way to strain agonizingly against the suspended weight of the body, every muscle taut, as though ready to fall if the nails were not holding it. But in another way the crucified figure seems to be holding the cross up, under great strain with the weight of it, but still managing to keep it elevated.

Commenting on the extraordinary technique in St. John's drawing, René Huyghe, Conservator in Chief of the paintings in the Museum of the Louvre, remarked as follows:

> Some people imagine that seeing is merely a matter of opening one's eyes. Seeing is a technique, a science which makes slow progress from century to century. There is a technique in vision just as much as in execution. . . . St. John of the Cross escapes right out of those visual habits by which all artists form a part of their period. He knows nothing of the rules and limitations of contemporary vision; he is not dependent on the manner of seeing current in his century; he is dependent on nothing but the object of his contemplation.[1]

From a cultural and historical standpoint, the distance between the sixteenth-century Spanish mystic St. John of the Cross and the twentieth-century Southern writer Flannery O'Connor is indeed great. One can of course point to their similarity as Catholic believers and even perhaps to some general influence of the Spanish mystic on O'Connor's work. But to help focus my study, I want to concentrate on the theme implicit in Huyghe's observations on the crucifixion sketch: the confluence of the religious and artistic sense within the artist. "Seeing is a technique. . . .

There is a technique in vision just as much as in execution." In the last analysis, at least with respect to Flannery O'Connor, I shall want to amend Huyghe's remark and argue for more of a unity between the techniques of vision and of execution than he seems to suggest. Notwithstanding this amendment, his comment helps shed light on several of the arresting and difficult problems in O'Connor's fiction that are the subject of my discussion.

The theme of my study, stated simply, is Flannery O'Connor's vision of history. No sooner is it stated, however, than a rush of problems of clarification immediately arise. Some would challenge the use of the term *history* itself, demanding to know what it means. The last eighty years have seen such a revolution in the way we regard the idea of history and so many different views have emerged that we are likely to feel, like Eliot's Gerontion, trapped in a baffling "wilderness of mirrors." Moreover, if we attempt to approach the question of O'Connor's vision of history strictly from the standpoint of deriving a philosophy of history, we can quickly find ourselves in the land of labels. Was she a millennialist? An apocalyptic? A Christian evolutionist? Was her view of history cyclical or linear? Such an approach, while interesting, is doomed to be only partially illuminating, because it is abstractive and therefore abuses the primary fact that O'Connor was first and foremost a writer of fiction. Consequently, any discussion of her vision of history not only will have to evolve from within the stories themselves but also will have to take account of the manner, the "technique in vision and execution," through which her ideas emerge.

What I am affirming, of course, is simply that the question of O'Connor's vision of history, as dramatized in her stories, is intrinsically bound up with the question of her practice as an artist. Once this fact is accepted, we are then faced with the difficult problem of understanding how the historical dimension actually comes into being and "works" in her stories, how she labors to create dynamic relationships between the past and the present within the action. But discussion of this problem presupposes a more fundamental question: the larger issue of the relationship between O'Connor's historical sense and her creative sense. Or to put the question more directly as an aesthetic issue: how does her historical sense function within the creative act? To raise this question is to push ultimately into the realm of metaphysics, for it seems impossible to me to discuss the matter, at least in O'Connor's case, without first trying to shed light upon her fundamental notions about the nature of being itself. All the crucial questions—about her vision of history, about the relationship between past and present, about her artistic practice—ultimately lead back to the metaphysical foundation: her radical sense of the order of reality.

Some critics have argued either implicitly or explicitly that O'Connor's sense of the order of reality is fundamentally Manichean.[2] For them, her vision is dualistic; furthermore, it is tipped by a preponderant weight on evil. My own belief is that this critical view cannot finally be sustained in O'Connor's case and that it is based upon an incomplete understanding of her metaphysics and its relationship to her artistic practice, at least in the major stories and novels. Critics who understand O'Connor's fiction to be Manichean suggest that a basic "division" exists between her avowed religious and conceptual artistic beliefs and her achieved practices as a writer. My own view, to the contrary, is that O'Connor's metaphysical sense, which derives from her Catholic belief, is the intrinsic foundation for both her vision of history and her artistic technique. Moreover, I assume her metaphysics, historical vision, and artistic technique all derive specifically from her belief in Christ's Incarnation and Redemption of human history—a belief which, ideally, made her historical sense and her artistic sense inseparable within the creative act. How this unity can be seen developing and operating in her stories will be the main burden of my study.

Before proceeding to examine in detail the basis of O'Connor's vision of history, I need to mention a further complication. There is a tendency among some critics of O'Connor's fiction to write about her work as though her vision remained essentially unchanged from the publication of her first major stories until her death. There is some justification for this assumption, given her avowed commitment to orthodox Catholic doctrine, the relative uniformity of her major work, and the fact that she referred to her development as a writer in terms of a "deepening" in the understanding and practice of her art. But such a view taken without careful scrutiny can produce a rather monolithic view of her work. On the other hand, it seems clear that considerable differences in artistic strategy and execution exist between, say, "A Good Man Is Hard to Find" and "Greenleaf" or "Parker's Back." These differences are undoubtedly a result of certain advances in O'Connor's sophistication as a writer—in handling tone and point of view, for example. But in the light of my thesis of the intrinsic relationship between her vision of history and her technique as a writer (both based in Christ's Incarnation), such differences raise another important question: what connection, if any, is there between O'Connor's development as a writer and her theological development? Does her vision evolve along with her technique, and, if so, what is the relationship between these two movements? The period during which she wrote her major works was one of profound and disturbing soul-searching within the Catholic Church, a period when the old scholasticism-based orthodoxy was being seriously reassessed and many attempts were being made to find a new theological language suitable to the religious problems of the mid-twentieth century. As we know from her reading, O'Connor avidly kept up with the new ideas and reassessments and constantly expanded her knowledge. Her studies ranged from traditionalists such as Gilson and Maritain to revisionists such as Rudolph Bultmann. Her wide reading was a process of "deepening" which is clearly evident, say, in her adaptation of the vision of Teilhard de Chardin in "Everything That Rises Must Converge."

Though her religious orthodoxy remained, I believe, essentially unchanged throughout her career, contemporary explorations of crucial questions—the impact of Christ on human history, modern concepts of the Christian imagination and Christian consciousness, and the problem of the "closure" of history, for example—had a significant impact on her thought and writing and therefore influenced the shaping of her art over the years. One of her chief problems as a Christian writer was how to get her vision across to an audience she considered to be largely indifferent, and "how to" necessarily involved technical decisions.

I do not want to suggest that there is a necessary or inevitable development in her artistic practice that corresponds uniformly to the development of her religious thinking. To do so smacks of a kind of artistic determinism, as if the writer's latest story were unquestionably the best or most sophisticated. In truth, some disjunction between religious vision and achieved fictional form does exist in some of O'Connor's work, as in the rather forced use of the Old Testament prophets motif at the end of "A Circle in The Fire." At this stage I merely want to introduce the question of her religious-artistic evolution as a vital issue for consideration, partly to emphasize the dynamic of her growth against the habit of seeing her thought and art in a totally monolithic way and partly to stress again my sense of the intrinsic relationship between her practice as a writer and her vision of history. To grasp this issue more clearly, I want to begin with a discussion of the metaphysical basis of her art, the precise point where history and the creative act interpenetrate.

The title *Risen Sons* derives from my belief that the Christian resurrectional vision forms the basis of O'Connor's treatment of character, theme, and history throughout her mature work. In addition, it points implicitly by way of pun to that image of divine power—the sun—which became a brooding presence in her fictional landscape.

The organization of this book is essentially thematic, as indicated by the chapter titles. At the same time, I have generally proceeded along chronological lines in discussing O'Connor's canon in order to anchor my arguments about the development of her vision of history. However, I have also done much crosscutting within the canon when appropriate to illustrate particular themes. Finally, I have assumed a knowledge of the basic action of O'Connor's fiction on the part of the reader and, for purposes of conciseness, have avoided unnecessary recapitulation.

Chapter One

The Metaphysical Foundations
of O'Connor's Art

The practical intellect knows for the sake of action.
—*Jacques Maritain*

Before undertaking a direct analysis of O'Connor's fiction, it is necessary
to offer some background remarks about the particular biblical view of
history, and its metaphysical foundation, that I shall argue shapes her
work to the core.[1] This will necessarily be a sketchy primer, but an important one to present for two reasons. First, there are often misconceptions
about basic ideas in her biblical view of history which are then carried over
into O'Connor criticism. Often there is a lack of precision in defining
certain crucial concepts like "mystery." Or again, first principles are assumed without examination or elaboration of their specific implications.
Ideas that have a precise meaning in O'Connor's biblical view of history—
and that she used with precise care in her essays, reviews, and stories—are
frequently invoked in a rather general or vaporized way, and thus their
exact sense is blurred.

The second reason for these background remarks is that O'Connor's
theology is often either assumed or treated in piecemeal fashion, even by
her most sympathetic critics. For example, the theology that informs her
fiction is rarely linked explicitly to her metaphysics, and her metaphysics
in turn is not often linked to her aesthetics. In the deepest core of O'Connor's thought and art, such a fragmentation is simply impossible. Theology, metaphysics, and art are intrinsically related in a single act of vision
and belief.[2] Such is the case, I believe, with the thought and its expression
in O'Connor's major work, and it will be the burden of this chapter to
show, conceptually, those main lines of intrinsic relation. Obviously it is
not intended as a full discussion of the particular biblical view of history
that informs her major work, but one that is nevertheless sufficient, I
hope, to reveal the core of ideas relevant to her art.

Some critics and readers, of course, may maintain that no matter what particular biblical view of history is cited and no matter how often O'Connor referred to it in her essays, letters, and reviews, it is not the same as what she *actually* wrote in the stories. The obvious implication in this critical view is that a breach exists between O'Connor's religious thought and her art, or that her fiction goes beyond the correspondences to her religious thought. There is a sense in which this is true, if by "beyond" we mean penetration into the world of mystery. However, to pursue this argument to the extreme conclusion that O'Connor "knew not what she wrought" or to suggest that she created works whose core is antagonistic to her religious thought seems to me simply untenable. Considering how highly self-conscious an artist she was and the enormous care and revision that went into her work, the evidence seems to argue otherwise.

Nevertheless, some critics suspect that reading O'Connor's work in the light of her religious thought may dangerously gloss over the deepest aspects of her work. Their suspicion, I would argue, is often the result of misunderstanding the meaning of that religious thought and its relation to her work. These critics regard her religious thought as monolithic and prescriptive and assume that O'Connor's relationship to it was an overtly static one of passive acceptance (with the corresponding implication that her imagination was therefore covertly subversive of this religious thought). This theory strikes me as a caricature of O'Connor as believer and artist. My own view is that her relationship to religious ideas was a dynamic agon and that this struggle marked her fiction every step of the way. To view her fiction in such a way is to see how it embodied those ideas and how the fiction itself came to be shaped by those ideas. Of course O'Connor was cognizant of the "cost" (one of her favorite terms) of her religious beliefs, but cognizance does not mean denial. The struggle over the cost is what we see in the fiction, and the final judgment about the value of my critical perspective must lie in how well such ideas illuminate the fiction. My first task is to discuss certain aspects of her particular biblical view of history which I think need to be focused clearly for consideration of her work. Only then can the way in which this view shapes, and is shaped by, the fiction be discovered.

The phrase "biblical view of history" is of course high-sounding, rather pontifical. It suggests in a popular sense a sort of universal, cosmic perspective of history, a grand providential design. In a sense this is accurate; but what needs to be emphasized here, because we are dealing with O'Connor *as artist,* is that the particular biblical view of history that informs her work is immediate, direct, and specific. In other words, a certain "historical" view in this biblical perspective means a way of looking at every specific object, every specific event, and it means a way of under-

standing their significance. Even the most common, humble, and everyday thing or act can be seen "historically" in this sense, because it is impossible to look at them without some idea of what they are, what they mean, and what they portend about existence. This way of seeing is both intensive and extensive. A simple object like a wooden leg or a peacock can be the medium of historical vision. Nothing is insignificant. This is the sense in which I use the word *history* in relation to O'Connor: to indicate a way of viewing and understanding the specific objects and actions she creates and to see how they are linked to her vision of history considered in its totality.

To help delineate the metaphysical foundation of O'Connor's vision, I want to begin with those fundamental themes identified by theologian Claude Tresmontant as central to biblical metaphysics in his *Study of Hebrew Thought*. First is the belief that this world has been *created* by God. The fact that genesis begins in a positive act and not by a "fall" or dispersion of the One into the Many is of absolutely crucial significance. It means that the created world is inherently good, that matter is good. Such a belief stands in direct opposition to a Manichean view of creation. Moreover, in this biblical view the sensible world, the world of nature, is intelligible; it can be known. Since its creation was by an act of the Word, its meaning can be discovered and named by man. In addition, because genesis was a positive act and because living things that have been created *are,* there exists in them no dualism of form and matter. As created beings they are existing entities: *"the biblical world is a world in which the idea of 'matter' does not occur"* (*A Study of Hebrew Thought*, p. 46). As a corollary, the dualistic notion of a body-soul dichotomy is entirely foreign to this biblical metaphysic, according to Tresmontant. The Christian distinction between "flesh" and "spirit" is an entirely different concept. In Christianity, "flesh" signifies the living person (body *and* soul) as part of the natural order; "spirit" signifies man's participation in the supernatural order. Finally, the idea of Christ's Incarnation is centrally rooted in this view of the created universe, the "goodness" of the sensible concrete world, and the nondualistic idea of being and of history. Created by the Word, the world then receives the divine Word in human form, a paradox inconceivable to dualistic thought.

Secondly, in this biblical view history is evolutionary: it has a beginning, a specific point of transforming apotheosis (the Incarnation), and a definite end (the Last Judgment). History's direction is therefore linear. Such a view subsumes the cyclical notions of history; it has subsumed and transformed the meaning of myth and mythic reenactment. Moreover, in this biblical view history is seen as dynamic and processive; all creation "groans" toward the new world to be born. The creative act that began history is ongoing; it is not an act that occurred once and is terminated, nor will it be terminated until the end of history. Since history began in a divine creative act, it follows that there exists no dualism, no division between the temporal and the eternal, the mundane and the supernatural. The notion of time signifies the process of becoming as it unfolds in creation throughout history. But it is not simply a measure of temporal progression; it signifies an ongoing creative act whose origin is divine. An event is therefore both a fact and a sign; it is a sign with meaning because it indicates the direction of the ongoing genesis of history, its movement toward maturation.

The central truth about reality under this biblical view is that of *mystery*. This concept, the linchpin of Christian theology, is frequently invoked by O'Connor herself and by her critics. However, its precise meaning has often been assumed, misunderstood, ignored, or glossed over in discussions of her work. Sometimes it is used to suggest mystification, obscurantism, or total impenetrability. But, according to Tresmontant, the biblical sense of mystery and of its implications is quite definite: "Mystery today means something impenetrable to the mind, something never to be understood. To St. Paul and to the early Christian thinkers it was on the contrary the particular object of intelligence, its fullest nourishment. The *musterion* is something so rich in intelligible content, so inexhaustibly full of delectation for the mind that no contemplation can ever reach its end. It is an eternal delectation of the mind" (p. 137). The crucial point to note is that mystery is intelligible; it is a proper subject of knowledge; it can be known *as* mystery.

Thirdly, in this biblical view metaphysics and the intelligibility of the world are united in the fact that creation came from a Word: "In the beginning was the Word. All was made by Him." Creation is a call, a call to being. Through the act of creation, "All sensible realities, all nature, have their principle in a word. For this reason they are essentially intelligible" (p. 52). Because a Word initiated sensible creation, things can be known and spoken and revealed in their essential reality. Thus the relationship between intelligence and the created world is one of creative dialogue. According to Tresmontant, "in the biblical world the sensible participates in the intelligible by the fact of creation. It is itself not only an image but also a subsisting reality. It is both being and sign" (p. 58).

Because the creation of the sensible world derives from the Word, there is an intrinsic unity between biblical metaphysics and biblical poetics. According to biblical metaphysics, the sensible world is essentially significant and intelligible; there is no division between the sensible and the intelligible. The relationship between the two is analogical. Through contemplation of the sensible object its essential reality can be known; it can be grasped both as a fact and as a sign. Under a dualistic notion of creation, the sensible lacks essential significance; it has no meaning in itself and it possesses significance only by virtue of its participation in the ideal world. Thus a division exists between the sensible and the intelligible: "Dualism disrupts analogy and it is analogy which is the principle of biblical poetics" (p. 62). Conversely, biblical poetics focuses upon the sensible, the particular, as a vehicle of meaning. At the metaphysical heart of this poetics of analogy is the doctrine of the Incarnation, in which the Word assumes a particular, concrete, historical identity:

> The Hellenic mind can never come to terms with the Incarnation, because of the antinomy which it places between the sensible, which is temporal, and the intelligible, which is timeless. Its Manichean conception of the sensible, its pessimistic conception of becoming, its view of time as a degradation of the timeless, its theory of individuation by matter and its ontology of the many and the one, and of the particular existent, all incline it to reject as unthinkable the coming into this world of Truth through a concrete, particular reality. Dualism is the contradiction of the method of the Incarnation. (p. 65)

The view of the person—his absolute ontological significance—follows necessarily from its metaphysics. Any dualistic conception of the person is therefore rejected. Any notion of individuation by matter, of spirit distinct from body, is impossible under this biblical view. A person is a living soul, absolutely unique and irreplaceable. Two profound consequences of this view of Christian personalism concern the notion of human freedom and the notion of evil. In this biblical idea of creation, God's making of man "in his likeness" means profoundly that man is made as a creative being with the power to choose his destiny. The freedom he possesses is essential to his nature as a creature; otherwise God's creation would be hollow and without ontological significance. Man would be the product of an act of sterile iteration, not a creature made through a free act of love and possessing freedom. A corollary to this belief is the notion that the origin of evil is not to be found in matter. Creation was neither a fall from the Godhead nor an act of alienation from the One. Since God's creation was a positive act and since the material was good at its inception, any dualistic notion under which matter is viewed as inherently evil is totally rejected. In the view Tresmontant outlines, the origin of evil is spiritual rather than material. All sin is a spiritual act. Evil is the result of a free choice made by the intellect, a choice in fact of what one's existence is to be. Thus evil is of the spiritual order and is real.

Because this biblical view of man is nondualistic and because biblical metaphysics allows no division between the sensible and the intelligible, understanding is not separated from action. The activity of the intellect— knowing and understanding—is not dissociated from the sensible or material world. Understanding, therefore, is not a passive faculty; it is an *activity* of the whole person: "Understanding *is* action, the act of intellection of subsistent truth" (p. 124). This concept of understanding is linked inherently to the belief in man's participation in the supernatural order; that is, through his spirit man is capable of receiving and responding to the truth communicated to his understanding by God: "The Biblical conception of understanding is tied to its anthropology, and particularly to its doctrine of the *pneuma*. Understanding, in the Bible, is a 'spiritual intelligence'" (p. 126). Thus Tresmontant defines the biblical notion of intelligence as a "creative intuition of Being in genesis," a perception of what things are and what they signify about the ultimate direction and meaning of events. Conversely, stupidity is closure, a lack or refusal of knowledge, and since understanding in this biblical metaphysics is tied to knowledge of the spiritual good, stupidity in this sense means a loss of the knowledge of God: "Lack of knowledge, unintelligence is a sin. It is *the* sin" (p. 128). "Knowledge of God is not purely speculative but an action incarnated in the world of men" (p. 128). This concept of understanding and of the unity of thought and action is extremely important for comprehending what actually *happens* to O'Connor's characters, what they choose in the mind, as we shall see later.

It is important to note briefly at this point how this biblical metaphysics radically affects the notion of salvation. Under dualistic systems of thought, salvation is often construed as a transcendence of matter, which is seen as defective; salvation is achieved by an escape from the body. Thus asceticism and stoic practices become equated with salvation, a way of rising above the contaminating limits of the physical. However, this biblical viewpoint rejects such practices as the means to salvation per se. Instead, salvation is regarded as spiritual. It demands a change of intellect, so that the mind is receptive to the understanding of the spirit. As St. Paul admonishes, "Do not conform to this world but be transformed by the renewal of the intellect . . . be renewed by the spirit of your mind."[3]

An inevitable implication of the biblical view of intelligence and understanding is that no opposition exists between reason and faith: "Faith, *pistis,* in the New Testament, is what the prophets called understanding and knowledge."[4] Since this biblical metaphysic is rooted in the unity of the sensible and the intelligible and since man possesses the power of "Spirit" to participate in the supernatural life through knowledge, faith and understanding are also united. But because this understanding partakes of the supernatural, faith is necessarily a mystery, an act of contemplation wherein men ascend to truth. This ascent is not by rejection of the physical, as in Greek thought; on the contrary, in the biblical view contemplation is intimately bound to the sensible, especially through the Incarnation. This view of reason thus contrasts sharply with a secularist view, necessarily so because of the Bible's affirmation of supernatural mystery, which can be known, as the proper object of intelligence.

Finally, this biblical vision identifies love as the absolute source and cause of all created reality. Since creation is seen as a continuing act of genesis of being, its reason can only be the proliferation of divine love. God created neither of necessity nor by a degradation from the One to the Many. This belief in divine love, according to Tresmontant, is the center of every aspect of biblical metaphysics: the belief that matter is inherently good and a subject of intelligibility; and the affirmation of Christian personalism, with its belief in human freedom, creativity, understanding, and man's participation in the supernatural through the spirit. More generally, the affirmation of divine love is the heart of a dynamic conception of history—history moving progressively toward its ultimate completion.

I have offered this brief overview or primer in an attempt to clarify some of the central premises in the biblical metaphysics, particularly its view of reality and history, that inform O'Connor's fiction. What warrants emphasizing here is the absolute unity that exists among the various aspects of this biblical vision; each aspect is intrinsically linked to all the others. Furthermore, it bears repeating that Flannery O'Connor's acceptance of this vision is not the case in point here. I would insist that O'Connor struggled with, in, and toward this biblical vision throughout the process of making her fiction. To understand this struggle we can begin by examining some specific implications of this biblical metaphysics within the creative act, both in a conceptual sense and by direct example from her fiction.

Flannery O'Connor's fiction is all of a piece. Probably more than any other American writer of her generation, she managed to create a coherent wholeness of vision and form; while all her stories are certainly not perfect, they seem to possess a kind of rocklike inviolability. Her major stories give the sense of being fully realized, whether the reader agrees with what they say or not. This quality of coherent wholeness has sometimes been difficult to perceive in critical discussions of her work. Readers who are sympathetic to her vision (and I obviously include myself among them) often tend to seize upon the great spiritual themes of her stories and elevate them in discussion to the point that, unwittingly or not, the manner in which they are realized is unduly subordinated to idea. This is a form of critical gnosticism that O'Connor, speaking from the standpoint of the writer, denounced in several of her essays, particularly "The Nature and Aim of Fiction": "The Manicheans separated spirit and matter. To them all material things were evil. They sought pure spirit and tried to approach the infinite directly without any mediation of matter. This is also pretty much the modern spirit, and for the sensibility infected with it, fiction is hard if not impossible to write because fiction is so very much an incarnational art." (*Mystery and Manners,* p. 68) Significantly, she focuses the fictional problem precisely in terms of metaphysics and theology. In the same essay, O'Connor views the problem from the standpoint of the reader's interpretation and argues for an approach based on an integral, organic view of fiction.

> People have a habit of saying, "what is the theme of your story?" and they expect you to give them a statement: "The theme of my story is the economic pressure of the machine on the middle class—" or some such absurdity. And when they've got a statement like that, they go off happy and feel it is no longer necessary to read the story.
>
> Some people have the notion that you read the story first and then climb out of it into the meaning, but for the fiction writer himself the whole story is the meaning, because it is an experience, not an abstraction. (p.73)

Other critics concentrate on various aspects of her technique—the comic, the grotesque, the hard style—and emphasize those features of her work. Still others express dissatisfaction with what the text *says* and, dismissing O'Connor's own ideas about language and its metaphysical base, attempt to decode the stories for implications in the language about the hidden impulses of the writer herself.

Many of these studies have been notable achievements in the effort to understand and appreciate her work. But they have also tended to obscure that fundamental quality of her work mentioned above—the coherent wholeness which gives her major stories their distinct integrity. This quality, of course, cannot fully be made the subject of intellectual analysis, since it involves the mystery of the creative act itself; nevertheless, it can be grasped as a mystery and made the subject of meditation. O'Connor herself insisted, following Aquinas and Maritain, that fiction writing is preeminently an exercise of the practical reason: "Art is a virtue of the practical intellect" (p. 81). But to comprehend something of the quality of wholeness in her work requires, I believe, some understanding of the metaphysical foundation of her art.

O'Connor insisted, as we have already seen, that the writing of fiction was an "incarnational art." What did she mean by such a phrase, as applied to her own work? The logical answer—one that any good fiction writer might give—is that story writing involves an imaginative process of incarnating the world's body in concrete language, using concrete sense images. This indeed was frequently the theme of O'Connor's statements: "The fiction writer has to realize that he can't create compassion with compassion, or emotion with emotion, or thought with thought. He has to provide all these things with a body; he has to create a world with weight and extension" (p. 92).

But language itself is symbolic—the word is not the thing—and this fact alone makes a phrase such as "incarnational art" problematic. Did O'Connor mean it only as a metaphor for the complex and ultimately mysterious process of writing? Perhaps in the popular sense she did. But the term *incarnational,* of course, also had a deeper, more specific resonance for her within the context of her Catholic theology. Given this context, she seems also to be suggesting a direct connection between the practice of "incarnational art" and a definite historical event—the Incarnation of Christ—*the* event in history which her fiction attempts to imitate.[5] Such a connection can be seen explicitly in her laudatory review of William Lynch's *Christ and Apollo: The Dimensions of the Literary Imagination:*

> In *Christ and Apollo,* Fr. Lynch describes the true nature of the literary imagination as founded on a penetration of the finite and limited. The opposition here is between Christ, who stands for reality in all its definiteness, and Apollo, who stands for the indefinite, the romantic, the endless. It is again the opposition between the Hebraic imagination, always concrete, and the agnostic imagination, which is dream-like. . . . The principle of this thorough penetration of the limited is best exemplified in medieval scripture exegesis, in which three kinds of meaning were found in the literal level of the sacred text: the moral, the allegorical, and the anagogical. This is the Catholic way of reading nature as well as scripture, and it is a way that leaves open the most possibilities to be found in the actual. (*The Presence of Grace,* p. 94)

How central this concept was to O'Connor can be seen from her incorporation of it into her own aesthetic in "The Nature and Aim of Fiction":

> The kind of vision the fiction writer needs to have, or to develop, in
> order to increase the meaning of his story is called anagogical
> vision, and that is the kind of vision that is able to see different
> levels of reality in one image or one situation. The medieval com-
> mentators on Scripture found three kinds of meaning in the literal
> level of the sacred text: one they called allegorical, in which one
> fact pointed to another; one they called tropological, or moral,
> which had to do with what should be done; and one they called
> anagogical, which had to do with the Divine Life and our participa-
> tion in it. Although this was a method applied to biblical exegesis,
> it was also an attitude toward all of creation, and a way of reading
> nature which included most possibilities, and I think it is this
> enlarged view of the human scene that the fiction writer has to
> cultivate if he is ever going to write stories that have any chance of
> becoming a permanent part of our literature. (*Mystery and Manners*,
> pp. 72–73)

I will discuss the precise character of O'Connor's anagogical vision of
history subsequently, but here I want to focus upon the roots of that vision
in the Incarnation of Christ. It seems clear that O'Connor's use of the
phrase "incarnational art" cannot be construed as simply a conventional
description of how the writer operates. Rather, it implies a whole way of
seeing reality, from the immediate concrete to the farthest reaches of
human history and beyond. More important, it implies an intrinsic relationship between the historical event of Christ's Incarnation, present-day
reality, and the creative act of fiction writing as O'Connor attempted to
practice it. Following Lynch, I use the term *intrinsic* in the philosophical
sense to indicate an essential *identity* between the nature of the two acts of
incarnation, the historical-Christian and the artistic, as I shall discuss
more fully later. Such an identity between Christ's Incarnation and the
creative act, when achieved, would mean that the form and technique of
O'Connor's best stories cannot truly be apprehended as distinct from her
vision of history, since her concept of creativity is rooted in what is for her
the axial event in human history. Conversely, the vision of history O'Connor embodied in the best stories is inseparable, then, from the manner in
which it is realized. What she attempted, it seems to me, is a total interpenetration of the Christian historical sense and the intuitive creative
sense in the act of writing fiction.

O'Connor derived the metaphysical basis for her incarnational aesthetic from many sources, but primarily from her understanding of St. Thomas Aquinas through the writings of Jacques Maritain, Etienne Gilson, William Lynch, and others.[6] While many aspects of Aquinian thought were important to her practice as a writer, the cornerstone of her aesthetic is to be found in the doctrine of the analogy of being because this concept conjoined her artistic practice with her vision of history within the creative act. We can begin to penetrate this complex mystery by consideration of a fundamental critical question: how is history—the evocation of the past—made to "live" in a work of fiction? More specifically, how did O'Connor make her Christian vision of history live within her stories, incarnating it so that it dramatically creates value within the work? For her stories to have that coherent wholeness I have claimed to be her goal, there has to be an interpenetrative relationship between theme and form in the way her vision of history is realized. To state the matter differently, the way in which history is "realized" in the story determines *both* its aesthetic and ontological validity.

This question—how the historical dimension is made to live in a work of fiction—cannot of course be answered solely by thematic analysis. Some works of fiction evoke history, and particularly Christian themes, as a kind of evaluative norm against which to measure the literal action; however, it is done in such a way that the history is static within the work. It is there as a constant referent (I use the term perjoratively) to which both author and reader make mental leaps in order to discover the "significance" of a particular action. O'Connor recognized and condemned such an approach several times in her book reviews; one "religious" novel she referred to as "fictionalized apologetics [which] introduces a depressing new category: light Catholic summer reading" (*The Presence of Grace,* pp. 72–73). In short, history evoked in this way is actually dissociated from the concrete level of action, imposed like an overriding scheme of values, and not generated dramatically from within the action itself. It fails to create in a specific way what Eric Voegelin describes as the "mystery of history," which for him is the essential drama of mankind.[7]

In other cases we often find Christian themes and images evoked in the story in such a way that their full mysterious reality is shrunken or deformed to fit the particular vision of the writer, a process which distorts or diminishes the historical analogue, usually by sentimentalization. Carson McCullers's character Mr. Singer in *The Heart Is a Lonely Hunter* is an example of such distortion, it seems to me. O'Connor herself was acutely aware of this problem in her own writing—the problem of how to render history as an analogical dimension of the literal action so that the history is both dramatically "present," while evoking the past, and dynamically creative of the depth of value carved into the work. The key to understanding this question, at least from a philosophical viewpoint, lies in the doctrine of the analogy of being.

As a metaphysical concept the principle of analogy of course has a long and complex history in the Western philosophical tradition. Full discussion of its development is beyond the scope of this study, particularly since as a concept of being the principle of analogy is at the heart of much contemporary discussion in theology, language theory, and aesthetics. Indeed, there is extensive, ongoing argument in theology and literary criticism over various interpretations of St. Thomas Aquinas's understanding and use of the concept. For example, in his brilliant study *The Story-Shaped World: Fiction and Metaphysics,* Brian Wicker argues that the medieval philosophical synthesis achieved by Aquinas and others overemphasized analogical language at the expense of metaphorical language, so that the concept of analogy fell into disrepute when the medieval synthesis came under attack.[8] Wicker attempts to revitalize and extend the Aquinian notion of analogy by linking it to the use of metaphor and metonymy in story; at the same time he affirms what he sees as the core of the scholastic notion of analogy: that a causal intrinsic relationship exists between the parts of the analogy. Most important, Wicker argues that the principle of analogy is as valid a metaphysical principle today as it was for the medieval scholastics, a point with which I think O'Connor certainly would have agreed:

> But what was true in the medieval period is still in principle true for our own time: the analogies themselves may have changed, and the repertoire of metaphors with them, but the analogical principle itself, and its capacity for generating metaphors, has not. For underlying the medieval "Great Chain of Being" was a causal conception—that of *creation*—which was simply another application of the relationship we have already encountered, between language and speech, between competence and performance, code and message, system and syntagm in the structure of human communication itself. Thus, the argumentative structure of Aquinas's "Five Ways" involves the notion that God's existence can be established from the existence of causal chains such as motion, or the coming-into-being and passing-away of things, by just the same sort of analogical reasoning which tells us that the utterance of a sentence, or the employment of a gesture *requires* the existence of a language, or a code of gestures. This is because the structuralist principle too

involves a *hierarchy of causes* just as the medieval world picture did: and while the exact form of the hierarchy is different, the consequences of this fact are fundamentally the same.[9]

On the other hand, in *The Analogical Imagination* David Tracy distinguishes between analogical and dialectical traditions of language; he shows that there are several traditions of the concept of analogy and argues that the tradition which developed from Aquinas abandoned the truly pluralistic ground of the principle of analogy in favor of a deadening, reified doctrine.[10] Tracy thus claims that the scholastic tradition of analogy lost its dialectical dimension, which he sees contemporary process theologians such as Karl Rahner and Edward Schillebeeckx attempting to revitalize through their theologies.[11] Siding with the process theologians, Tracy's study is a brilliant attempt to reconcile the analogical and dialectical traditions; like Wicker's, it emphasizes the validity of the analogical vision. This vision, for Tracy, is centrally rooted in the "focal event" of Christ.

While Tracy is undoubtedly correct in his criticism of those who reified Aquinas's notions of analogy into formula, his concern is primarily with the tradition of theological language and not with the language of the artist. My own view, developed in the next chapter, is that O'Connor fully retained the dialectical dimension of analogy in her practice of image-making in the major stories. Consequently my discussion of analogy here closely follows that developed by Lynch in *Christ and Apollo,* particularly because Lynch focuses on the *literary* implications of the doctrine of analogy as related to the historical event of Christ's Incarnation and because O'Connor knew Lynch's work well.

In its popular sense the term *analogy* may denote simply the practice of making metaphorical associations by drawing likenesses between different objects or actions—for example, the simple metaphor "the heart is a dark cavern," which points implicitly to the qualities both objects possess. Although this kind of analogizing is indispensable to the writer, the parallels it suggests are fundamentally extrinsic to the objects or actions being linked. In the philosophical sense on the other hand, we shall see that the notion of analogy describes an *intrinsic* relationship between the nature of the objects or actions themselves. An inherent similarity of form, or structure of being, thus exists between two objects or between, say, the actions of old Mason Tarwater in *The Violent Bear It Away* and Christ.

The doctrine of the analogy of being is a metaphysical answer to the problem of how being can be everywhere both alike and different. Consequently, this doctrine attempts to explain the structure of all existence by avoiding the two extremes of viewing existence in a univocal way (every-where the same) or in an equivocal way (everywhere different):

> The act of existence descends analogously, *ana-logon,* "according to a proportion." The degree of existence is always measured by the degree of possibility, by the degree of fullness of being any possibility may receive. The form of a mouse can receive only so much. No one yet knows how much the form of man can hold. But the proportion is always one and the same and altogether unvarying. It is always a proportion of "existence according to possibility." That has always been and always shall be. It is an absolute invarient. All being is therefore one and the same, completely predictable and with a decision which never changes as it advances in its processes. . . . Existence, as it descends, is analogous. It is never the same act of existence. It is a completely new fact; it must be new; for it must adapt itself completely to the new materials which it confronts, adapting itself in its bone and heart to the bone and heart of each new subject of being, each new part of the total organism. So too with an analogical idea, with our inward thinking about being. The work, the thinking of it, is never done. The process of adaptation is eternal. We can never come up with one logical core and say it will satisfy the requirements of all the subjects. Only the proportion is the same; but the two parts of the proportion are always changing. The act of existence is always different; so too is the possibility, the material into which it enters.
>
> In other words, in an analogical organism of unity and its epistemological counterpart, an analogical idea, every thing in the subjects is always the same, and every thing altogether different.[12]

Lynch comments further about one of the implications of this doctrine that seems to me particularly relevant to a view of the relationship between O'Connor's belief and her art:

> It is this identity of act between the contraries in analogy which makes both for its obscurity and its glory. Its obscurity: for it is impossible to abstract the same from the different so that they become two clearly demarcated univocal ideas. Its glory: for it is through this obscure but actual interpenetration that by living in the world of men, with all its weaknesses, we can live with knowledge in the world of God. We need not utterly change our ways and thoughts to know Him; we need not utterly jump out of our

skins to get to Him. *If analogy is a fact, then we need have no religious or imaginative resort to Manichianism.*[13]

The doctrine of the analogy of being, I would argue, describes from a philosophical viewpoint how a certain historical analogue—classical, biblical, or otherwise—can be "present" in an authentically creative way *within* the literal level of a story. The historical analogue, rooted in the writer's deepest sense of the meaning of history, is part of the "act of existence" descending and being realized proportionately "according to the possibility" of being within the concrete literal action. What is important to note is that the historical analogue is not attached to the literal in a simply external way, though of course this can occur too. Rather, there is an intrinsic similarity of structural form between the two levels in order for them to be properly interpenetrative and mutually illuminating. Otherwise the two levels are joined in a univocal way, so that the similarities drawn between them are arbitrarily imposed rather than developed dramatically from within the concrete. The historical analogue seems tacked on, causing a disproportion between the two levels. It is forced, and the reader senses the contrivance.

This distinction can perhaps best be illustrated by two examples: one from Faulkner's writing, in which the historical analogue seems to be present in a dissociated, univocal way; and a second from O'Connor's, in which the historical analogue germinates dramatically from within the literal level. In the first example, the "temptation" scene from *A Fable*, the priest draws an analogy to the historical Christ while trying to talk the doomed corporal out of his sacrificial gesture:

> "The Book," the priest said. The corporal looked at him. "You mean you don't even know it?" "I can't read," the corporal said. "Then I'll cite for you, plead for you," the priest said. "It wasn't He with his humility and pity and sacrifice that converted the world; it was pagan and bloody Rome that did it with His martyrdom; furious and intractable dreamers had been bringing that same dream out of Asia Minor for three hundred years until at last one found a Caesar foolish enough to crucify him. And you are right. But then so is he (I don't mean Him now, I mean the old man in that white room yonder onto whose shoulders you are trying to slough and shirk your right and duty for free will and decision). Because only Rome could have done it, accomplished it, and even He (I do mean Him now) knew it, felt and sensed this, furious and intractable dreamer though he was. Because even He said it Himself, *On this Rock I found My Church,* even while he didn't—and

never would—realize the true significance of what he was saying, believing still that he was speaking poetic metaphor, synonym, parable—that *rock,* meant unstable inconstant heart, and *church* meant airy faith. It wasn't even his first and favored sycophant who read that significance, who was also electrocuted by the dreamers intractable fire, like Him. It was Paul, who was a Roman first and then a man and only then a dreamer and so of all of them was able to read the dream correctly and to realize that, to endure, it could not be a nebulous and airy faith but instead it must be a *church,* an *establishment,* a morality of behavior inside which man could exercise his right and duty for free will and decision, not for reward resembling the bedtime tale which soothes the child into darkness, but reward of being able to cope peacefully, to hold his own, with the hard durable world in which (whether he would ever know why, or not wouldn't matter because now he would cope with that too) he found himself. Not *snared* in the frail web of hopes and fears and aspirations which man calls his heart, but *fixed, established,* to endure, on that *rock* whose synonym was the seeded capitol of that hard durable enduring earth which man must cope with somehow, by some means, or perish. So you see, he is right. It wasn't He nor Peter, but Paul who, being only one-third dreamer, was two-thirds man and half of that Roman, could cope with Rome. Who did more; who, rendering unto Caesar, conquered Rome. More; destroyed it, because where is that Rome now? Until what remains but that *rock,* that citadel. Render unto Chaulnesmont. Why should you die?" (pp. 364–65)

Although rhetorically grand and certainly important from a thematic standpoint, this passage from *A Fable,* does not achieve the kind of dramatic analogical movement of the literal and historical together, interpenetratively, which a fully realized passage would achieve. It lacks what O'Connor described in "The Nature and Aim of Fiction" as "anagogical vision." It has the ring of rhetorical embellishment; the rhetoric is heightened to help "explain" the meanings latent in the action. But this heightening temporarily, and fatally, draws our eye away from the concrete situation. The meaning is imposed on the situation through rhetoric, rather than growing from *within* the action. The literal sense and the historical analogue being evoked are *disincarnated;* to use Lynch's term, they are linked in a univocal way. Thus while Faulkner's prose is unquestionably powerful, the reader senses a disproportion between the two levels.[14]

Contrast this passage with one from O'Connor's "A Temple of the Holy Ghost," a "revelation" scene at the end of the story:

The chapel smelled of incense. It was light green and gold, a series of springing arches that ended with the one over the altar where the priest was kneeling in front of the monstrance, bowed low. A small boy in a surplice was standing behind him, swinging the censer. The child knelt down between her mother and the nun and they were well into the '*Tantum Ergo*' before her ugly thoughts stopped and she began to realize that she was in the presence of God. Hep me not to give her so much sass. Hep me not to talk like I do. Her mind began to get quiet and then empty but when the priest raised the monstrance with the Host shining ivory-colored in the center of it, she was thinking of the tent at the fair that had the freak in it. The freak was saying, "I don't dispute hit. This is the way He wanted me to be."

As they were leaving the convent door, the big nun swooped down on her mischievously and nearly smothered her in the black habit, mashing the side of her face into the crucifix hitched into her belt and then holding her off and looking at her with little periwinkle eyes.

On the way home she and her mother sat in the back and Alonzo drove by himself in the front. The child observed three folds of fat in the back of his neck and noted that his ears were pointed almost like a pig's. . . .

Her mother let the conversation drop and the child's round face was lost in thought. She turned it toward the window and looked out over a stretch of pasture land that rose and fell with a gathering greenness until it touched the dark woods. The sun was a huge red ball like an elevated Host drenched in blood and when it sank out of sight, it left a line in the sky like a red clay road hanging over the trees. (*Complete Stories*, pp. 247–48)

This passage, it seems to me, achieves a deeper analogical realization of meaning than the Faulkner passage from *A Fable*. We note first of all O'Connor's strict adherence—her fidelity—to the literal details of the scene, to *observed* reality. This is presented without rhetorical embellishment; it speaks for itself. Vision and meaning are united, not separated, and made to grow from within the action. As the scene unfolds, the action proceeds with a point-by-point correspondence between the literal level and the "history" being evoked through it without jumping off from the concrete. We have a fully concretized dramatic movement—the child's change of mood and her mental association of the benediction service, the hermaphrodite at the carnival, and human grotesqueness. Within that same movement, evoked through it analogically, we have an image of the historical Christian Incarnation, the Host, united to nature in the form of a hierophany, the Host-like sun "drenched in blood" as it sets beyond the treeline. Unlike the passage from *A Fable,* the historical analogue here is so fully concretized within the action of the scene that it gives greater validity to and receives validity from the literal level, *in the present*; the action moves forward to dramatize meaning. In the Faulkner passage, action is stopped to discuss meaning; in the O'Connor passage, there is a dynamic of reciprocal insight operating between the two levels. One reads the words and the literal action (the movement of the child's mind) is both "same" and "different" from the historical analogue (the movement or incarnation of the divine into the things of this world). Yet the reader experiences the two movements analogously because of the intrinsic unity of form between the two. In philosophical terms, we have the same princi- ple of proportion—existence according to possibility—operating within the literal and the historical levels and in relation to each other analo- gously. In the passage from *A Fable,* however, the reader does not experi- ence the same unified, concrete dramatic movement of the historical and the literal. Their linkage is compelled by force of rhetoric, and the link remains extrinsic.

The most significant difference between the Faulkner and O'Connor passages is in O'Connor's ability here to create the sense of *mystery.* Both passages evoke historical, theological analogues, but Faulkner's is directly explicit and self-conscious; it prescribes a certain meaning to the passage which paradoxically vitiates its significance. O'Connor, on the other hand, creates vision implicitly through the details of the passage—the Host, the freak, the nun's crucifix, Alonzo's pig ears, the sun, the trees. O'Connor preserves the mystery of the scene by leaving it to the reader to envision the "connection" between the literal details and the hierophany, and she thereby respects both the created fictional world *and* the reader. She re- fuses to assign meaning arbitrarily and explicitly, as Faulkner does in *A Fable.* In short, O'Connor creates Voegelin's "mystery of history," *suggesting* extensions of meaning through the literal by carefully adhering to the analogical principle in the act of writing.

The question of *how* the historical dimension is realized in an authen- tically analogical way in fiction is a mystery within the creative act; it is bound up with the historical sense, the incarnational sensibility, and the nature of the free act itself. Nevertheless, the principle of analogy gives several important clues both to the dynamics of this process and to the deeper sense which can be implied from O'Connor's use of the phrase "incarnational art." First, if the historical dimension is realized analogically in a work, there can be no question of a simply metaphorical, extrinsic relationship between the history evoked and the concrete literal level. Since analogy of being is based on a law of proportionality, an intrinsic relationship must exist between the historical and the literal into which it descends. The same formal structure of being must be common *to the nature* of both parts, though each is really a different thing: "It is easy to see that in the case of univocal thinking it is a relationship of unqualified externality. But in analogy the relation is one of unqualified penetration."[15] So it is not a question of fitting the historical analogue to the concrete, nor of heightening the concrete to match the dimensions of the historical analogue. The concrete is narrow, limited, and, one might think, not large enough to contain the many and complex movements of the historical which are being evoked. But as we shall see later in our discussion of the impact of Christ's Incarnation on the structure of being, one mystery of analogy is that, as Lynch explains, the limits of possibility of being within the concrete are never exhausted by the act of existence. Moreover, the central paradox of analogy is that only through fidelity to the concrete can analogical vision be fully realized. O'Connor certainly had this realization in mind when she said of the creative process: "It seems to be a paradox that the larger and more complex the personal view, the easier it is to compress it into fiction" (*Mystery and Manners*, p. 73).

A second important characteristic of the analogical is that the relationship between the historical and the literal in a work is not static or passive. As Lynch notes, the heart of analogical movement is dynamic and dramatic action: "*action* is the soul of the literary imagination in all its scopes and forms, and . . . metaphor either springs out of action as one of its finest fruits, or is itself one of its many forms" (*Christ and Apollo*, p. 155). In the passage quoted from "A Temple of the Holy Ghost," the reader does not just intellectually observe the different levels of meaning unfold throughout the passage, as I think occurs in the passage from *A Fable*. Rather, he experiences through the language the same dramatic structural movement incarnated in the passage. Thus history descends into the literal, the literal in turn validates that history, and the two levels interact dynamically. Or to state the matter differently, their relationship is one of mutual and continuing revelation, each incarnating the form and meaning of the other in a dramatic and ongoing way. Lynch demonstrates this process at work in the Old Testament narrative of the Jews' liberation from Egypt:

> The Jews of the Old Testament are liberated from Egypt and from the waters of the Red Sea. This is more than just a word, it is also

an historical fact. Yet without becoming less of a fact, it is also a sign, a type, of another reality to come, the liberation of Christ from the dead. Yet it is more than an historical metaphor, or an artificial sign implanted in a fact, chosen at random to be related to something else. For it has the same concrete structure, though on a poorer and less important level, as that greater thing toward which it points. And the deeper one goes into the whole historical concretion of the earlier reality the more insight there is into that which is to come. . . . But the reverse is also true. If one brings the Resurrection back over against the liberation of this ancient people from the waters, that first act of liberation is illuminated as never before. There is a mutuality of forces for insight operating between the two events. Each is borrowing light from the other. (*Christ and Apollo,* p. 184)

The process here described by Lynch seems to me precisely that which is operating in the passage quoted from "A Temple of the Holy Ghost," and it is a manifestation of the "anagogical vision" that O'Connor held as an ideal for the fiction writer.

I would argue that the doctrine of the analogy of being in O'Connor's case is specifically related to her redemptive vision of history. In noting that the biblical idea of intelligence is "a dynamic intuition of Being in genesis," Tresmontant has demonstrated the connection of incarnation, anagogical vision, and the historical perspective implicit in the Judeo-Christian heritage:

In Platonism the sensible participates in the Idea by a degradation. . . . In the Biblical universe, the sensible participates in the intelligible by creation. . . . It is at one time being and sign. . . . The Platonic symbol for representing and signifying a metaphysical or theological reality appeals to a myth, to the unreal. The symbol is disincarnated. The sensible, the concrete, is not suitable to carry the message. It is necessary to construct a chimera.

On the contrary, the Hebrew uses daily things, communal reality, history, to signify and teach the mysteries which are the proper nourishment of the spirit. . . . The advantages of the Hebrew method of teaching metaphysics and theology by the *maschal* and the parable of concrete fact is its capacity for universality. The *maschal* grows from the concrete, the most common, the most universally human. . . . In the Biblical mode of expression, it is enough to be human to understand that which is proposed. The Biblical parable is as intelligible for the Galilean peasant as for the

Corinthian docker in the time of St. Paul, as it is for the workers in
the factories of Paris in our time. A Greco–Latin culture is often an
impediment to an understanding of these parables, which imply a
sense of the real and of work, and such a love of the concrete
element as seems a defect to the Platonic mentality; the latter is
more or less unconsciously dualist, and too aristocratic to prove the
depth and richness of the mystical content of these daily realities of
working with the elemental. . . . The particular is the existent.
Hebrew thought springs from the particular existent; the particular
in the Biblical universe is neither negligible nor insignificant. [16]

Tresmontant's description of this particular biblical view of creation corresponds to O'Connor's insistence upon anagogical vision for the writer in
"The Nature and Aim of Fiction." When achieved, this vision enables the
writer to reveal history in a truly creative way. It is not a matter of revealing a history which unravels in time according to some preexisting plan;
this would be Platonic imitation instead of creation. Rather, in this particular vision, creativity and the historical sense are rooted in the Christian idea of human freedom, so that the artist may authentically "create"
the universe in all its material and spiritual reality. O'Connor constantly
reinforced such a notion in her essays, particularly in "Catholic Novelists
and Their Readers":

There is no reason why fixed dogma should fix anything that the
writer sees in the world. On the contrary, dogma is an instrument
for penetrating reality. Christian dogma is about the only thing left
in the world that surely guards and respects mystery. The fiction
writer is an observer, first, last, and always, but he cannot be an
adequate observer unless he is free from uncertainty about what he
sees. Those who have no absolute values cannot let the relative
remain merely relative; they are always raising it to the level of the
absolute. The Catholic fiction writer is entirely free to observe. He
feels no call to take on the duties of God or to create a new
universe. He feels perfectly free to look at the one we already have
and to show exactly what he sees. He feels no need to apologize for
the ways of God to man or to avoid looking at the ways of man to
God. (*Mystery and Manners*, p. 178)

While the doctrine of the analogy of being provided the general metaphysical basis for O'Connor's vision, the specific character of her aesthetic-
historical sense derived from a belief in Christ's Incarnation: "I see from
the standpoint of Christian orthodoxy. This means that for me the mean-

ing of life is centered in our Redemption by Christ and what I see in the world I see in its relation to that" (p. 32). As Lynch points out, moreover, with the Incarnation the crucial question for the believer-artist now becomes: what radical effect on the structure of being, with its analogical principle of "existence according to possibility," is caused by Christ's immersion into human history? We recall that in analogy there is a proportionality between the act of existence and the form it actuates, an intrinsic relationship between the two parts. But in the case of Christ's Incarnation—divine existence actuating human form—the proportionality, or possibility of being, is radically altered. This is one of the meanings of the Misfit's remark that "Jesus thown everything off balance." What new level of being is introduced, and what new intrinsic structural identity can be seen to exist between the human and divine natures? Lynch states the problem of the Christological dimension as follows:

> In our chapter on analogy, we saw that it was an act called existence which was descending deeper and deeper into the possibilities of the world to take on the proportions of those possibilities while retaining an identity. Nothing stopped it from remaining the same; no difference was lost through being organized by it. This is the action of creation, and of the endless dynamisms set in motion within the created world.
>
> Yet there has been a second and new creation. And now the form which shapes it is no longer an existence which becomes different in everything it touches, leaving only the proportion the same, the proportion between the act of existence and the possibility of the essence. Now the action is Christ, rigidly one person, born in that place, at that time, with all those specificities, with this body. How energetic (and esemplastic) will he be, how malleable to him will the world be? . . . It is now demanded of a new imagination that it use this "hopelessly rigid" form as a new analogical instrument with which to enter into the shapes of all things without canceling them out. . . . For Christ, we have said, is not another item of the first creation, to be used as any other item by the old imagination. The real point is ever so much more crucial. For he has subverted the whole order of the old imagination. Nor is this said in the sense that he replaces or cancels the old; rather, he illuminates it, and is a new level, identical in structure with, but higher in energy than, every form or possibility of the old. (*Christ and Apollo,* pp. 185–87)

With Christ's immersion into history, a new dimension is added to the analogical. There is still the proportion of "existence according to possibility," but because the act of existence descending is greater—the divine Christ—the possibilities of being are immeasurably increased. No one knows how much. The relationship between Christ and human history is an analogical one: he descends as the energy of existence to fulfill perfectly all the possibilities of being within history. Christ himself is an analogical power which shapes creation and history and gives them their deepest meaning. The uniqueness of Christ as an analogical instrument is that he is a single, concrete, historical person who claims to be the new shape of all things, yet he does not change by being realized in different things in creation, nor are they obliterated. The different elements and acts in creation and history are gathered up in him and linked together meaningfully. His analogical union with creation is complete; it fulfills all the possibilities in existence, such as time, death, rebirth, mystery, identity, and the hypostatic union of spirit and matter. This is the mystery of the Incarnation. With this total analogical identity of a specifically historical Christ and specific human history, things and acts in creation are raised to a new level of meaning, and the precise sense of the concept of Providence becomes clear: that everything in existence "counts"; nothing is neglected in the redemptive perspective. As O'Connor herself noted, nothing in creation is inconsequential for the Christian writer. Lynch concludes: "Thus Christ is water, gold, butter, food, a harp, light, medicine, oil, bread, arrow, salt, turtle, risen sun, way, and many things besides."[17] This is not simply metaphorical expression; it proclaims the intrinsic metaphysical identity between Christ and creation brought about by his Incarnation into history.

A crucial implication in Lynch's view of the Christological, particularly as it affects the writer, is that the relationship between Christ's Incarnation and the "new" creation is not static. Though rooted in a definite historical event and a specific time, the relationship is dynamic and ongoing. Consequently, it is possible to speak of a process of "Christianization" of matter and consciousness through cooperation with grace—the redemptive process. O'Connor's affirmation of this process can be seen clearly in her review of Teilhard de Chardin's *The Phenomenon of Man* and of Claude Tresmontant's study of Teilhard:

> In his early years Teilhard was oppressed by a caricature of Christianity, one to a large degree prevalent today in American Catholic life, which sees human perfection as consisting in escape from the world and from nature. Nature in this light is seen as already

fulfilled. Teilhard, rediscovering biblical thought, "asserts that creation is still in full gestation and that the duty of the Christian is to cooperate with it. . . ." Tresmontant points out that asceticism in Teilhard's view no longer "consists so much in liberating and purifying oneself from 'matter'—but in further spiritualizing matter. . . ." Teilhard believed that what the world needs now is a new way to sanctity. His way, that of spiritualizing matter, is actually a very old way. . . . It is the path which the artist has always taken to his particular goals. . . .

His is a scientific expression of what the poet attempts to do: penetrate matter until spirit is revealed in it. (*The Presence of Grace*, pp. 87–88, 130)

This process of spiritualization does not mean that the existent thing merely transcends its limited form. In fact, the effect of Christ's Incarnation is the opposite under analogy. Rather than subsume or obliterate the identity of existing things, it allows them to be deepened more fully in self-identification, to become what they truly are. There is nothing inevitable or deterministic about this process. While Christ's Incarnation brings a new possibility for being into existence, which in theological terms would be called the action of grace in nature, the glory of human freedom includes the possibility of rejection and the choice of evil, as several of O'Connor's characters clearly demonstrate.

Thus far, my discussion of the metaphysical basis of O'Connor's technique and vision of history has necessarily proceeded along theoretical lines. Now I want to offer a specific illustration from her fiction of the practical operation of this metaphysic. The three most obvious paths need to be avoided, paths which present more problems than real insight into the functioning of her metaphysic. First are those instances in her stories when characters, such as the Misfit or Father Finn or Mason Tarwater, make direct reference to the Christian tradition; second, instances when the narrative voice itself directly injects a Christian perspective, as in the ending of "The Artificial Nigger" or *The Violent Bear It Away;* and third, instances when O'Connor uses direct allusions, such as references to Tobias, Virgil, and the Holy Ghost, to deepen the significance of the literal action.

Theological speeches such as the ironic "prophetic" vision of Mrs. Shortley in "The Displaced Person" represent only a particular character's point of view and not necessarily the author's. In any event, these instances are too obvious and narrow to reveal O'Connor's metaphysic at work in the total movement of the story. The direct narrator comments may represent a weakness or lapse in the author's aesthetic; some critics have argued that O'Connor occasionally overstepped the plausible bounds of the story in her zeal to make the audience see clearly the import of the action, as in the ending of "A Circle in The Fire." And direct reference to biblical or classical persons or to theological concepts, though vitally important in the stories, are insufficient *by themselves* to create the kind of historical meaning through analogy that O'Connor sought in her fiction. In short, to understand the operation of her metaphysic as a way of seeing and creating the historical dimension in her stories, one must concentrate directly on the dramatic movement of the story itself, since *action*—being in genesis—is at the core of the analogical vision and the Christian historical sense.

What can we identify as the "typical action" in O'Connor's stories, one that illustrates the analogical both as fictional technique and as embodiment of her historical vision? To present this essential action I want to focus on the Grandmother in "A Good Man Is Hard to Find" as a prototype, although one of a host of other characters could easily be substituted: Mrs. Shortley, Julian, Asbury Fox, Ruby Hill, Hulga Hopewell, or Mr. Head. First of all, it seems obvious that the Grandmother begins in an ahistorical state of gnosis or detachment from reality, a state in which she truly does not know herself. In her case this state is engendered by her sentimental attachment to a nostalgic, distorted vision of the past. Consequently, the initial action involves some kind of *descent* for the character, almost always brought about by a kind of violence. This movement of descent is analogical, and the action imitated is in fact an incarnation, a movement toward knowledge of the true self. One may wish to call this action by the traditional term, a *fall,* or use a metaphor from another O'Connor story and call it a *displacement.* The Grandmother's rude displacement from her lofty vision of herself as a morally superior "lady" is brought about by her meeting with the Misfit.

But what does this action of descent produce? We might say that the action which the Grandmother is embarked upon places her on a "downward path to wisdom"; however, remembering the impact of Christ's entrance into history, we might more appropriately call it a downward path into "possibility." That is to say, what this action of descent produces in the Grandmother is a new and radical realization of the full possibility of human beingness, the kind of possibility for free *action* created by Christ's descent into and transfiguration of history.

To put the matter concretely, the descent which the Grandmother undergoes creates in her, first of all, a new vision of the order of reality. But what characterizes the order of reality she experiences is mystery; there is always more than can be fully apprehended by the human intellect. She is led to face what is so often the central question attending the "fall" in O'Connor's stories: what does it mean to be a person in history, *in this moment?* In other words, at the heart of the new vision received by the Grandmother is a sense of her true self—her total being—in relation to history, specified by her sense of her relation to history's child, the Misfit. But here too mystery reigns. There is always "more to" the person than the self in the immediate moment; the Grandmother must face the mystery within her own being, something she has not done before. This is the mystery of human "possibility" created by Christ's entry into human form, "thowing everything off balance." Similarly, under the doctrine of analogy and the mystery of freedom, the Misfit as antagonist embodies *both* demonic and Christlike potentialities. There is always more to the present historical moment than the immediate physical situation; the present moment embodies the mystery of history in which each moment contains, analogically, the absolute and the infinite, a fact signified by the Misfit's remark: "She would of been a good woman . . . if it had been somebody there to shoot her every minute of her life."

Finally, the new vision which the Grandmother receives as a result of her descent—since it involves implicitly the action of grace—culminates in a profound sense of *choice,* an awareness of the absolute human freedom to act creatively in a new way vis-à-vis history. This sense of choice is shown in the Grandmother's gesture of acknowledged bond and communion with the Misfit just before her death. But the true choice, and the heart of its mystery, is not to transcend history. The choice implied in the Grandmother's gesture toward the Misfit is one in which she follows the path of the Incarnation—into the broken world, embracing history—an action that testifies paradoxically to man's ability to rise through grace as the "New Man" by descent into his full humanity. The Grandmother, then, recapitulates the action of the Incarnation at the human level. Consequently, analogical movement and historical vision are enacted in the story, and the story itself becomes a dynamic revelation of the mystery of history.

The doctrine of the analogy of being, as I believe this example illustrates, provided the metaphysical basis for O'Connor's practice as a fiction writer. It was central to her aesthetic because it gave a philosophical foundation to the kind of typological fiction she aimed to write—with one action conveying several layers of meaning. But most important, it provided a coherent unity between her technique and her vision of history—between fictional incarnation and *the* Incarnation—and thus, I believe, enabled her to create that unique wholeness which is such a distinctive feature of her work.

Chapter Two
Beginnings: Seeing and the Search for the Incarnational Image

Belief, in my own case anyway, is the engine that makes perception operate.

—*O'Connor's comment on her own work*

Although she was not a professional theologian or philosopher, O'Connor was obviously deeply influenced as a writer by her considerable reading of traditional and modern Christian scholarship. This reading confirmed her own belief and practice, and it shaped her aesthetic viewpoint indelibly. More specifically, as I have suggested, the doctrine of the analogy of being provided a metaphysical underpinning for her fiction. It offered a systematic way of viewing reality and its dimensions, which extend into mystery. Moreover, the concept of the analogy of being is totally consonant with the Christian vision of history, for, as Lynch has shown, it is rooted in the metaphysics and meaning of Christ's Incarnation. In this view, a single image can embody or contain a full vision of reality and history, resonant with all its implications. Yet while this belief clearly informed O'Connor's approach to fiction writing, the realization of the vision developed slowly in actual practice. It was a task that would occupy the author for the rest of her creative life, not always with success. As her art matured, so did her awareness of the difficulties inherent in creating the kind of vision she wished to convey. The essential problem remained the same throughout her career: how to create images that would "connect" the Incarnation with fictional incarnation, Mystery with mystery—the "two points" of light which she attempted to incarnate within a single dramatic image.

In the earliest stories O'Connor wrote there is little sign, either explicit or implicit, of the Christian historical vision that developed in her mature work. With the possible exception of "The Turkey," her first five stories might well have been written by any gifted young writer, though there are a few hints of distinctive themes that come to be realized fully later. Not until she began to work on the Hazel Wickers/Hazel Motes material which became the subject of *Wise Blood* did she seem to "discover" her true subject and begin to develop fictional strategies to embody it dramatically. In writing the story of Haze, O'Connor achieved a breakthrough in vision by which she was able to present the literal action in terms of the larger Christian vision of history. Equally important, however, is the fact that she began to discover *how* to present this vision analogically, so that one action or image might convey multiple dimensions of meaning. In short, I would argue that the breakthrough O'Connor achieved involved a simultaneous discovery of the Christian historical vision as a fictional subject and of the analogical method as a fictional strategy; together, these constitute the definitive characteristic of her mature work. In writing Haze's story she began to move toward that fictional ideal of anagogical vision she upheld in "The Nature and Aim of Fiction" and explicated in various ways throughout her book reviews and essays. [1] A review of the early stories and the sharp departure O'Connor took from them in writing Haze's story reveals this transforming development in her vision.

"The Geranium" (1946) contains no definable suggestion of a Christian vision of history conveyed analogically through the literal action. Old Dudley, the protagonist, is a southerner living with his daughter in New York City. Cut off from his native roots, he feels trapped in the alien world of the urban North. His situation and his memories of the South enable O'Connor to suggest the conflict in values between the anonymous, hostile city and the traditional society of the South. But this conflict is presented faintly, and essentially in social terms. Nothing in the story suggests that the "southern" values represented by old Dudley should be seen in a larger Christian historical perspective, a characteristic of O'Connor's more mature work in which southern material is transfigured into a larger theological/historical context. Moreover, her use of the theme of memory in "The Geranium," dramatized in Old Dudley's reveries of "back home," is undistinguished from many other southern writers' use of this theme: memory is a mode of ordering the chaos of modern experience. [2] In later works, as we shall see, O'Connor also transfigured this southern theme within the context of Christian eschatology. Finally, the narrative technique in "The Geranium" is essentially straightforward and linear. Nothing in the structure of the story suggests the kind of vertical deepening, the fusion of the linear and the cyclical, which is so characteristic of the analogical view of reality and the Christian vision of history. Nevertheless, given the inherent possibilities in the story's basic situation, it is not surprising that O'Connor would return to it near the end of her career in "Judgement Day," recasting it in terms of a Christian providential vision of history—death and final resurrection.

"The Barber," written sometime before 1947, introduces Rayber, a weak, disgruntled intellectual who is the prototype of a long line of gnostic "thinkers" O'Connor came to portray in her fiction, including of course the antagonist in *The Violent Bear It Away.* The relationship of mind to reality—to the world, to history, and to the possibilities of a transcendent order—was to become one of the most significant themes in her mature work. In "The Barber" it is essentially undeveloped. There is nothing to suggest any deeper implications to Rayber's peevish disgruntlement beyond his own bumbling ineffectuality, which O'Connor exploits mainly for comic purposes. Similarly, the racial theme is cast mainly in social terms; it is not presented with the profound theological and historical dimensions she gave it in "The Artificial Nigger" and later in "Everything That Rises Must Converge." In "The Barber" the action is focused in the present only and in terms of social realism. The story's strength is in O'Connor's fidelity to detail and her comic sense. But these elements are one-dimensional here and lack the resonance of historical depth.

"The Wildcat," also written sometime before 1947, suggests the beginnings of important new developments in her fiction insofar as it shows her conscious attempt to introduce a religious dimension into the action. In the waiting of the old blind Negro for the coming of the wildcat, there are faint suggestions of the prophetic theme of the Old Testament. The language of the story is more explicitly religious, and more important, dramatic tension builds in such a way as to suggest an almost apocalyptic inbreaking of divine power:

> "Lord waitin' on me," he whispered. "He don't want me with my face tore open. Why don't you go on, Wildcat, why you want me?" He was on his feet now. "Lord don't want me with no wildcat marks." He was moving toward the cat hole. Across the river bank the Lord was waiting on him with a troupe of angels and golden vestments for him to put on and when he came, he'd put on the vestments and stand there with the Lord and the angels, judging life. (*Complete Stories,* p. 31)

The sense of mystery is stronger in this story than in either "The Geranium" or "The Barber." In addition, Gabriel's name, his blindness, and O'Connor's attempt to depict something of his inner consciousness all suggest her groping toward a deeper fictional vision. This vision is not fully coalesced or articulated in "The Wildcat," particularly because the central image of the wildcat is not developed with sufficient dramatic precision and concentration to embody the religious dimension O'Connor wants to signify by it. She had not yet clearly focused the "two points" of illumination between the literal and the anagogical, but she was moving closer.

"The Crop" (pre-1946) introduces what became a familiar O'Connor theme: the comedy of the would-be writer whose romantic pride precludes any success as a creator. Miss Willerton leads a rich fantasy life, but her detachment from the common world, a world suitable as a proper subject for fiction, makes any real creativity impossible. O'Connor's serious point is clear: the necessity for the writer's hard commitment to the real, concrete world if any higher vision is to be extracted, a commitment marked by struggle, suffering, and frequent defeat. Such a commitment, of course, strongly suggests the incarnational view, the analogical movement downward into the world of matter, opposite to the kind of gnostic detachment that incapacitates Miss Willerton (and Asbury Fox, Julian, and Calhoun later). Nevertheless, O'Connor's emphasis in "The Crop" is on satiric portraiture rather than extended implication of meaning. Miss Willerton's story is not linked to any larger historical perspective, Christian or otherwise; later, treating the same theme in "The Enduring Chill" and "Everything That Rises Must Converge," O'Connor does make this connection.

"The Turkey" is the most significant of the early stories for what it anticipates of O'Connor's developing vision and fictional strategy. Ruller's capture and subsequent loss of the injured turkey to a group of mean country boys is the backbone upon which O'Connor builds a small drama of the child's initiation into the world of mystery. Wandering alone, Ruller fantasizes about having power over the world and achieving heroic stature in his family's eyes by capturing a turkey. But the real world turns out to be a trick which constantly frustrates his fantasy. Significantly, Ruller identifies this trickery with God and rebels against Him in his mind, swearing and speculating about how he might "turn bad" like his older brother Hane. But when Ruller surprisingly captures the turkey, there is a comic reversal and he fantasizes God to be a kindly benefactor for whom he wishes to do something, like give a dime to the poor. But God is not to be manipulated quite so easily; when his turkey is stolen by the mean boy, Ruller is harshly thrust into the real world of experienced mystery—that "Something Awful" which pursues his running figure at the end of the story.

Several notable innovations make "The Turkey" substantially different from the other early stories. For the first time the story's drama involves a direct, extended treatment of the protagonist's relationship to the divine order. Equally important is the fact that much of the drama is centered in Ruller's consciousness; O'Connor's focus, as Frederick Asals has shown, is upon the sin of rebellion which is "of the mind."[4] Her emphasis here introduces what became a major theme in her work, the theme of deceptive consciousness; the mind's capacity for distortion in apprehending the real and its proneness to closure when impinged upon by the divine. Ruller's condition anticipates O'Connor's later development of the theme of gnosis and closed consciousness in characters such as Hulga Hopewell, Mr. Head, Mrs. McIntyre, Mrs. May, Rayber, Sheppard, and others. The boy's mental attempts to manipulate God also foreshadow those self-serving inner visions of characters like Mrs. Shortley and Mrs. Turpin. Finally, O'Connor ends the story on the note of the intrusion of mystery. The dramatic movement of the story is more distinctly analogical, in the sense that analogy means an incarnational movement into a reality whose extensions of meaning extend beyond the literally comprehensible.

"The Turkey" still ranks as juvenilia, in spite of these real advances in O'Connor's art. For one reason, her depiction of Ruller's character is relatively simple, compared to the later complexity of Nelson or Young Tarwater. Ruller's inner fantasy of rebellion against God is treated too slightly; it lacks the theological depth O'Connor engendered in the mental struggles of later child protagonists. Moreover, the relationship of Ruller's rebellion against and manipulation of "God" to the revelation of mystery, the "Something Awful" at the end of the story, is not dramatically unified. This relationship might have been realized through the use of a strong hierophantic image to focus meaning; however, the turkey possesses none of the "extensions of meaning" suggested by the hermaphrodite, the peacock, or the statue of the artificial nigger. Nevertheless, "The Turkey" is distinctly an O'Connor story, possessing clear trademarks of her emerging vision. It is hard to imagine another American writer having written it.

When O'Connor turned to the story of Hazel Wickers/Motes, however, she came to discover the true subject of her fiction—man's relationship to God and his struggle over redemption. This discovery, it would appear, involved intimations about the problems of *how* to write as well as *what*: "You discover your audience at the same time and in the same way that you discover your subject; but it is an added blow" (*Mystery and Manners*, p. 18). This remark suggests her awareness of the enormous difficulties of conveying her subject to a largely indifferent audience, an awareness leading to her conscious adoption of the grotesque as a fictional strategy. What bears particular emphasizing here is O'Connor's understanding of the intrinsic link between her vision and her method; the "true subject" of her work was defined as much by how she presented things as by what she presented. Her understanding points directly to the link between theology and art, between Incarnation and incarnation, and especially to the relationship between the doctrine of analogy and the grotesque. How?

Analogy, as we have seen, means existence according to possibility, a proportion which has been altered immeasurably by Christ's entrance into history. In this view, all men are "grotesque" insofar as they contain the possibility of redemption, yet fail to realize it fully. At the same time, this condition of "grotesqueness" defines the dimensions of real human nature. On the other hand, what O'Connor found to be "grotesque" in the modern world was its attempt to deny the true spiritual grotesqueness of man, a denial made by rational and gnostic claims to human self-sufficiency. Man can achieve wholeness by his own natural efforts, the age seems to claim. But this vision of a balanced and fulfilled humanity is in fact a vision of closure from the divine. Paradoxically, by denying his true spiritual grotesqueness, man also denies his possibility for becoming the New Man through spiritual transformation and transcendence. O'Connor's chosen task as a writer was to pulverize this false condition of closure through distortion, to destroy the specious "wholeness" of man by exaggerating the gap between his actual self and his potential spiritual self. Thus her use of the grotesque was firmly rooted in the doctrine of the analogy of being in its Christological form. The grotesque as a literary device is a tool that measures the dimensions and possibilities inherent in a given form of existence; through distortion, it implicitly signifies what is proper to the true nature of a person or thing.

When O'Connor discovered her true subject in the Hazel Wickers/Motes stories, her fictional vision was fundamentally altered and took on a power and depth of significance previously unimagined. Literal action now began to be conceptualized in terms of the larger historical framework of man's fall into sin and the need for Christian redemption, a new viewpoint which radically changed the formal qualities of her art as well.

"The Train," written before 1947, seems similar in tone and substance to the early stories already considered, except for the notable introduction of Haze Wickers and his haunting past. Journeying by train to Taulkinham from abandoned Eastrod, Haze cannot escape the memory of his lost roots and his dead mother. After suffering through a chaotic day on the train in which he is insulted and then rebuked by a Negro porter whom he tries to connect to Eastrod, Haze retires to the coffinlike sleeping berth, where he recalls his mother's funeral and the coffin lid closing down over her dissatisfied face. Haze imagines that his mother will fly up and prevent the lid from closing. But his vision of a resurrection is only a fantasy; the lid closes, death is final, and Haze awakens to find himself "sick" in the berth.

O'Connor's preoccupation with the death/resurrection theme in "The Train" represents a new departure in her fiction. Here the comedy is more serious than in the earlier stories, and understandably so, because O'Connor was moving toward the main theme of Christian comedy as it comes to face the absurd—the theme of death and thus the whole meaning of man's existence. Death was central to her creative imagination, as she remarked later, and comedy was most serious and comic when it measured the eternal reaches of man's capacities and activities. Additionally, there are important structural innovations in "The Train" that forge an analogical link between the action and the theme of the story. By recalling his mother's death, Haze is drawn backward by memory into a strong link with the past; this memory scene develops into a dynamic interaction (in both Haze and the reader) between recollected past and present action which is largely absent from the other early stories. In short, O'Connor began to exploit the thematic possibilities of structural discontinuity—of flashback, retrospection, and doubling of images and scenes. While such discontinuity represents a rather obvious complicating of her technique, what is not so obvious is the link between this strategy and the emerging vision of reality and history it implies. In O'Connor's case this retrospective technique is grounded in an analogical view of reality, a belief in the intrinsic likeness of things under redeemed creation. The incarnational *action* of analogy becomes the model for connecting two "points" of experience, such as Haze's present sickness and his obsession with his mother. Thus the dramatic movement of the story involves a vertical deepening of meaning within its linear progression, since "The Train" ends with Haze's move backward in consciousness to his mother. But because it ends where it does, the story likewise involves a cyclical pattern which suggests an analogical view of the meaning of human action and implicitly of the meaning of history within a cosmological order.

These implications are not fully developed by O'Connor in "The Train," although the seeds of future development are certainly planted in the story. Haze's mother is in no way connected with the Christian vision of sin and redemption, as she explicitly is in "The Peeler." Consequently, the true source of Haze's angst is vague, attributable only to natural causes—his sense of rootlessness, plus the rather transparent obsession with his mother. His "sickness" is presented exclusively in psychological, not theological, terms; what sense of mystery exists in the story is natural rather than supernatural. Moreover, Haze's story is diluted by O'Connor's mutual interest in Mrs. Hozen, a passenger who serves as a comic foil to Haze's bumptious provinciality. Finally, with the exception of the conventionally handled coffin image, the story lacks any symbol developed sufficiently to contain the several layers of meaning characteristic of the analogical capacity to incarnate mystery, especially the numinous. In sum, "The Train" lacks any fully developed religio-historical dimension.

Such is not the case in "The Peeler," published in 1949. Here one can see clearly a major breakthrough in O'Connor's fictional vision, for the story gives explicit, if somewhat slight, treatment to the theme of Christian redemption. At the same time, it attempts ways to make supernatural mystery concrete in the action. Although they have identical given names and superficial resemblance, Haze Wickers of "The Train" and Haze Motes of "The Peeler" are profoundly different characters. In "The Peeler" Haze's angst is clearly related to his obsession with sin and Jesus' redemption, the central mystery of Christianity, even though Haze attempts to deny this obsession when confronted by the preacher Asa Shrike. Moreover, in dramatizing Haze's attempted denial, O'Connor developed what eventually became the central image in all her major fiction: seeing and vision, sight and blindness. The image of "seeing" takes on many nuances throughout her work, of course, but in the deepest sense it indicates that power of vision through which her characters understand themselves and their place within the order of the cosmos, within history, and thus their grasp of the meaning of existence. In her stories, viewpoints—ways of seeing—range from the mechanistic/naturalistic to the providential/redemptive. Without oversimplifying, it is important to note the close correspondence between O'Connor's own struggle as a writer and that of the central characters in her major works—the struggle to see the concrete reality before them with all its extensions of meaning, through the literal and into the mysterious. In this respect, all her fiction, reflexively, is about the mystery of seeing, and the situation of the young girl in "A Temple of the Holy Ghost" is a paradigmatic representation of the artist's struggle: how to "see" the link in meaning between the concrete literal reality of the hermaphrodite and the divine-incarnated-in-flesh signified by the Eucharist. Another way of stating the problem, of course, is to say that it involves a struggle to develop an analogical and Christological way of looking at reality.

In "The Peeler" Haze Motes adamantly rejects any vision that would place him within a redemptive schema of history. Nevertheless, his final failure to claim innocence in *Wise Blood* is foreshadowed at the end of "The Peeler" when he recalls his mother's rebuke for his "sinful" visit to a carnival sideshow to see a woman in a coffin:

> "What you seen?" she asked, using the same tone of voice all the time. [We note that the emphasis is on what he has *seen*, not where he has been or what he has done.] She hit him across the legs with the stick, but he was like part of the tree. "Jesus died to redeem you," she said.
> "I never ast Him," he muttered. (*Complete Stories,* p. 80)

The next day Haze performs the penitential act of filling his shoes with rocks in order to evoke a sign from heaven; but no sign appears, and the story ends with Haze's abandoning atonement altogether.

It is difficult to underestimate the importance of "The Peeler," especially the final scene between Haze and his mother, as indicative of the way O'Connor discovered her true subject and began to realize ways to represent it. It can be called a breakthrough, because little in the other early stories quite anticipates its power and significance. It was not simply a matter of using the theme of sin and Christian redemption. Rather, the breakthrough in vision shaped every aspect of her work. In "The Train," for example, the Oedipal theme and the woman/coffin/death motif are expressed in terms of their natural, psychological significance. In "The Peeler," however, this same theme and motif are elevated to the level of supernatural mystery by being focused within a vision that sees action in terms of the central historical event of the Redemption. Moreover, this elevation is achieved without canceling out the value of the literal and psychological levels. O'Connor's drive to create this multidimensionality is underscored in her well-known comment to a friend that, in *Wise Blood,* Haze's actions are qualitatively different from those of Oedipus. The latter represent natural mystery, the former supernatural mystery. The capacity to embody these different levels of meaning in one image or action is of course the central feature of analogical vision. With "The Peeler," O'Connor began to create this added dimension.

The new focus of vision is evident in O'Connor's change of fictional strategies in "The Peeler." It was not a matter of experimentation in technique or of radical departure from her earlier stories but of deepening and broadening what she could do. In characterization, for example, Haze Motes is much more fully realized as a personality—as a mysterious presence—than his predecessor Haze Wickers, largely because the former concentrates fiercely on the ultimate religious significance of his life. Haze Motes is both more serious and more comic, his fanaticism focused in terms of an inverted Christian comic vision. This fanaticism is counter-pointed by the foil, Enoch Emery, whose behavior is comic on the natural rather than on the religious level. Enoch embodies all the predictable determinism of the natural order against which Haze's mysterious identity shines forth.

Second, there is a deepening of image and symbol in the story which is essentially unprecedented; images are created with a density that suggests mystery. The seeing/blindness/vision motif is developed with multivalent significance: Asa Shrike's literal blindness, Haze's blindness to his own sin, Asa's insight into Haze's obsession with Jesus, the fatuous blindness of Enoch Emery and Leora Watts, Haze's perverse insight into the folly of the world, and so on. The pattern is developed with such range of implication as to defy schematization. It is doubled and echoed with variation in such a way that structural and thematic unity is enhanced precisely *because* such repetition and transformation of images derive from analogical vision. As a result, the entire dramatic movement of the story becomes an analogical *action,* concretizing main elements in the Christian historical vision.

The best illustration is the conclusion of the story, when Haze recalls his mother's rebuke that "Jesus died for your sins" after his visit to the carnival sideshow. The placement of this recollection at the end is crucial. The action moves forward in linear fashion through Haze's day in the city—his meeting with Enoch Emery, the peeler salesman, Asa Shrike and his daughter Sabbath Lily, and his return to Leora Watts—and ends with a circular movement back to his past in the memory of his fall into sin and the knowledge of redemption. There is, of course, a fictional logic to ending the story with a revelation scene that unites all the preceding actions. But this is not just *any* revelation; it is radically different from Haze Wicker's recollection of his mother in the coffin in "The Train." The final revelation in "The Peeler" is a hierophany which transfigures the meaning of the action into a higher vision of reality in ways that the ending of "The Train" cannot achieve. The action at the conclusion of "The Peeler" not only evokes the idea of Christ's Incarnation thematically but also imitates that action formally. Haze's recollection of the judgment scene with his mother does not take the form of a mental reverie; O'Connor instead dramatizes it as though it were happening in the present. By rendering the scene in the present, she creates not just correspondences but also an intrinsic unity of form—an *imitatio Christi*—between past and present, and this difference represents a major advance in her vision and method.

Another way to shed light on this difference is to consider O'Connor's technique in comparison with other contemporary fiction writers. Her

suspicion of radical experimentation in fiction, especially the kind prac-
ticed by so-called post-modernists, is well known. In comparison to
Pynchon, Barth, and other experimentalists, her technique is conser-
vatively traditional. She avoided any attempt to "spatialize" narrative, to
use Joseph Frank's term, along postmodern lines or to undermine the
inherent consecutiveness of narration.[4] Her rejection of this kind of experimentation was not simply a matter of temperamental differences or
even of restriction to what she could do. As Frank and others have shown,
attempts to spatialize narrative are intrinsically related to and reflective of
the collapse of traditional metaphysics and the rise of modern skepticism.[5]
The radically altered sense of the metaphysical order of reality which proceeds from the postmodern viewpoint serves to undermine the traditional
meaning of time and action in narrative and often leads to the modes of
absurdism and solipsism in art and the view of narrative as simply an
autonomous "language construct" with no real relationship to experience
outside the text. O'Connor rejected all such tendencies. Her adherence to
traditional narrative structure derived from a metaphysical belief in an
inherent and discoverable order and meaning of reality—and a belief in
fiction as an instrument for revealing the truth of that order. This order
involved seeing the analogical-metaphysical relationship between, as she
put it, common everyday life on the Oconee River in Georgia and the
dropping of the atom bomb or, one might add, the "common" event of
Christ's entry into history two thousand years ago and present-day experience: "So far as I am concerned as a novelist, a bomb on Hiroshima affects
my judgment of life in rural Georgia, and this is not the result of taking a
relative view and judging one thing by another, but of taking an absolute
view and judging all things together" (*Mystery and Manners,* p. 134).

The significance of "The Peeler," then, in contrast to the other early stories, lies in its dramatization of a Christian historical vision and in O'Connor's use of the analogical principle as a unifying instrument of technique
and vision. This discovery of the dimensions of her historical vision, I
would argue, formed the basis for the shaping of all her major stories and
novels. It gave no easy or reassuring perspective from which to write,
however. On the contrary, it placed more formidable demands upon
O'Connor, a fact demonstrated by her intense concern with the problem of
creating the incarnational image and reflected in her direct statements as
well as the stories of her first collection, *A Good Man Is Hard to Find.*
Before turning to these stories, I want to focus again on the literary problem of image-making to show how O'Connor understood its relationship
to metaphysical belief.

The heart of the doctrine of analogy, we recall, is *action*, a dynamic interpenetration or dramatic movement by which meaning emerges through the image. Under the Christian view of analogy described by Lynch any specific image is theoretically capable of containing the many levels of meaning demanded of it. An image can represent the literal world and yet resonate with extensions of meaning that touch upon the mysterious and the transcendent, such as the statue of the artifical nigger. If the image embodies the transcendent, it is because of the natural object's capacity to be infused with divine grace. In such a case, the analogical action by which this occurs is transfiguration. The natural image then becomes a vehicle of grace and of revelation. The image's value as image depends upon how it is "seen" by characters and readers, and how it is "seen" is directly linked to the vision of reality and history it implicitly embodies as an image. In O'Connor's major work, the analogical action is linked to the specific historical event of the Incarnation. The incarnated image, in its fullest development, becomes an image of the Incarnation. Moreover, the analogical action of image-making also involves the mystery of freedom, since through artistic transfiguration the image is a natural sign—concrete and limited—with a significance "freed" from the confines of the natural order alone.

Although she did not express it in the language of metaphysics, O'Connor was concerned constantly with this problem of the metaphysical dimension of image-making—a concern reflected in her numerous essays and remarks. Speaking about the writer of grotesque fiction, she said: "He's looking for one image that will connect or combine or embody two points; one is a point in the concrete, and another is a point not visible to the naked eye, but believed in by him firmly, just as real to him, really, as the one that everybody sees" (*Mystery and Manners,* p. 42). Commenting on "Good Country People," O'Connor extended her explanation of how one image can embody "two points" of meaning in reference to Hulga's wooden leg:

> In good fiction, certain of the details will tend to accumulate meaning from the action of the story itself, and when this happens they become symbolic in the way they work. . . . The average reader is pleased to observe anybody's wooden leg being stolen. But without ceasing to appeal to him and without making any statements of high intention, this story does manage to operate at another level of experience, by letting the wooden leg accumulate meaning. Early in the story, we're presented with the fact that the Ph.D. is spiritually as well as physically crippled. She believes in

nothing but her own belief in nothing, and we perceive that there is a wooden part of her soul that corresponds to the wooden leg. Now of course this is never stated. The fiction writer states as little as possible. The reader makes this connection from things he is shown. He may not even know that he makes the connection, but the connection is there nevertheless and it has its effect on him. As the story goes on, the wooden leg continues to accumulate meaning. The reader learns how the girl feels about her leg, how her mother feels about it, and how the country woman on the place feels about it; and finally, by the time the Bible salesman comes along, the leg has accumulated so much meaning that it is, as the saying goes, loaded. And when the Bible salesman steals it, the reader realizes that he has taken away part of the girl's personality and has revealed her deep affliction to her for the first time.

If you want to say that the wooden leg is a symbol, you can say that. But it is a wooden leg first, and as a wooden leg it is absolutely necessary to the story. It has its place on the literal level of the story, but it operates in depth as well as on the surface. It increases the story in every direction, and this is essentially the way a story escapes being short. (pp. 98–100)

To understand the function of the wooden leg in relation to analogy and the implied vision of history, we need only consider how the leg is viewed in the story. In Hulga's skewed vision (and again we note O'Connor's focus on the seeing/blindness theme), the leg as object has been elevated to the status of an idol, with Hulga "taking care of it as someone else would his soul." That is, the leg as object has been *disincarnated* by Hulga, made in her eyes more than it really is by an intellectual act of false transcendence. She has imputed to it an ontic value which it does not possess. Similarly, she has made an idol of herself, signified by her act of renaming herself. In short, Hulga's actions reverse the proper analogical movement, for by making the leg and herself "more than they are" she has actually made them less. To view the leg and herself as Hulga does involves an act of metaphysical misplacement, a gnostic refusal to see the object and herself as they really are. Therefore, Manley Pointer's theft of the leg, as perverse as it seems, is in fact a destruction of the false idol which literally has come to embody Hulga's false vision of reality. The stealing actually precipitates an incarnational movement, leaving Hulga at least open to a new way of seeing things—most important, of seeing herself as a confounded, contradictory, yet mysterious human creature in history and not the detached, self-conceived disincarnated idol she had tried to make of herself. Manley's theft of the leg has in fact made Hulga potentially free.

O'Connor's use of the wooden leg as symbol, then, is based upon a larger theological perspective rooted in the Incarnation and implying a whole way of seeing reality as concrete, yet freely open to transfiguration. On another occasion O'Connor quoted with approval Baron von Hugel's remark that "the Supernatural experience always appears as the transformation of Natural conditions, acts, states" and that "the Spiritual generally is always preceded, or occasioned, accompanied or followed, by the Sensible. . . . The highest realities and the deepest responses are experienced by us within, or in contact with, the lower and lowliest." O'Connor added: "This means for the novelist that if he is going to show the supernatural taking place, he has nowhere to do it except on the literal level of natural events, and that if he doesn't make these natural things believable in themselves he can't make them believable in any of their spiritual extensions" (*Mystery and Manners*, p. 176). Von Hugel's statement and O'Connor's application of it to fiction-writing point to the fact that for her the mysterious intrusion of grace in nature is centered upon the transfiguring action within the concrete image, as in "A Good Man Is Hard to Find":

> I often ask myself what makes a story work, and what makes it hold up as a story, and I have decided that it is probably some action, some gesture of a character that is unlike any other in the story, one which indicates where the real heart of the story lies. This would have to be an action or gesture which was both totally unexpected; it would have to be one that was both in character and beyond character; it would have to suggest both the world and eternity. The action or gesture I'm talking about would have to be on the anagogical level, that is, the level which has to do with the Divine life and our participation in it. It would be a gesture that transcended any neat allegory that might have been intended or any pat moral categories a reader could make. It would be a gesture that somehow made contact with mystery. . . . Now the lines of motion that interest the reader are usually invisible. They are lines of spiritual motion. And in this story you should be on the lookout for such things as the action of grace in the grandmother's soul, and not for the dead bodies. (pp. 111–13)

Thus the anagogical action in the story dramatizes for her the mystery of freedom, the manner in which the natural order is transfigured by the divine. In response to a question about predetermined characters in fiction, O'Connor said:

I don't think any genuine novelist is interested in writing about a world of people who are strictly determined. Even if he writes about characters who are mostly unfree, it is the sudden free action, the open possibility, which he knows is the only thing capable of illuminating the picture and giving it life. So that while predictable, predetermined actions have a comic interest for me, it is the free act, the acceptance of grace particularly, that I always have my eye on as the one thing which will make the story work. (p. 115)

Each of these statements by O'Connor—on mystery, freedom, the action of grace, the transfiguration of nature—all point in slightly different ways to the same artistic problem: to find ways to create the incarnational image, the image which could serve as a vehicle of grace, of freedom, of mystery, and of vision. Hence her focus upon an object—geranium, turkey, car, statue, wooden leg, peacock, bull, or tattoo—as the medium of revelation. I say "vision" because her concentration on the object as hierophantic image is inseparably linked to the notion of "seeing." How her characters and her readers see specific objects is the defining point of their vision of reality and of history. Do they see the objects anagogically, as mysteries which contain the potentiality of the divine within nature? Are the objects seen as dramatic and potentially transformative signs of dynamic creative movement within a redemptive view of history? Or conversely, are they seen only as mundane objects, inert "things" that possess only material significance, made by man in the image of natural man? Such a view implies a vision of history which is mechanistic, static, and governed by closure, without any point of contact with a transcendent order. These two viewpoints are the contending visions of history in O'Connor's fiction, and the struggle between them is centered on perception of the significance of the image or object.

Throughout the first collection of stories, one can see this struggle and O'Connor's growing ability to embody it using incarnational images. One of the weaknesses of "The Turkey," I have suggested, is that the central object—the turkey itself—is not sufficiently developed as an image to contain the hierophantic dimension O'Connor wishes to convey in the story. Ruller manipulates the idea of God in his mind self-servingly, but this distortion is not convincingly linked either to the action of losing the turkey or to the "Something Awful" that haunts Ruller. As an image, the turkey is undramatic (inert and untransformable), and it lacks anagogical depth. This weakness is apparent when the turkey is compared with the peacock in "The Displaced Person." As an object the peacock explicitly embodies and focuses opposing visions of history. To Mrs. McIntyre the peacock is just a worthless "peafowl," a superfluity in her practical vision of the world. But to the priest, the bird is an image of a redeemed universe, a world filled with dynamic potential for redemptive transformation. As an image the peacock is far more successful than the turkey for two reasons. First, it is linked explicitly to characters' ways of viewing reality and consequently to the theme of seeing. Second, it is successful because linked *by analogy* to the central meaning of the action involving Mr. Guizac, which on the level of action is itself an image of the possibilities of transformation in history.

It is proper to speak of Mr. Guizac as an image in the story, because his function is drawn primarily in terms of the way he is seen by others; as an image, he is even more centrally linked than the peacock to the dramatic action of the story. Mrs. McIntyre holds essentially the same view of him as she does of the peacock, and for her the displaced person finally becomes a disposable object when he threatens to upset her closed world.[6] As an image, however, Mr. Guizac is analogically identified with the quintessential displaced person—Christ—who also upset the mundane order of history. Because Guizac's presence on the farm shatters the complacent world Mrs. McIntyre tries to create for herself, which is neither her true condition nor the true end of historical process, he finally comes to represent the mystery of history. In him O'Connor successfully creates an image of the possibilities of transfiguration in concrete, dramatic terms, even though these possibilities are rejected by Mrs. Shortley and, less assuredly, by Mrs. McIntyre. O'Connor had progressed a long way from the relatively simplistic image-making of Ruller and the turkey.

Developing the incarnational image was never a particularly easy task for O'Connor, and "A Circle in the Fire" suggests some of the inherent difficulties. One constant danger was authorial intrusion—forcing the analogical significance onto the specific image so that the meaning was "tacked on" and did not emerge from within it dramatically. Such is the case, I believe, in her linking of the three delinquent boys with the Old Testament prophets at the end of the story, a linking that seems precipitate and arbitrary. Though the main action of the story—the destruction of Mrs. Cope's pagan materialistic "kingdom"—generally supports the typological connection of the boys with the prophets, their function as prophetic instruments does not emerge from within the total dramatic movement of the story. The final paragraph of the story consequently comes as an unexpected shock.

A more successful handling of the problem of image-making can be seen in the complex analogical linkage O'Connor creates among the hermaphrodite, the Holy Eucharist, and the setting sun in "A Temple of the

Holy Ghost." The story's title and the physical condition of the hermaphrodite point directly to the mysterious relationship between the physical and the spiritual, the body and the spirit. More specifically, they point to the mysterious action of the *indwelling* of the spirit in matter—the incarnational action whereby divine spirit transforms the material world. The focal image of this mysterious process is the Holy Eucharist which the girl observes in the chapel. The host itself embodies the analogical principle by representing the mystery of transubstantiation, the indwelling of Christ in bodily form.[7] By analogy O'Connor thus connects the hermaphrodite's condition with the central image of the process of redeeming the physical world—Christ Himself. It is an image which also points to the transformed meaning of history, since the Eucharist is a historical referent to the human Christ who lived in history and who continues to be present in the Eucharist. In short, the story's central images are a microcosm of the analogical view of reality and history; as a consequence, the vision of the story is firmly anti-Manichean. Finally, O'Connor extends the range of meaning at the end of the story by the analogical link between the sun and "an elevated Host drenched in blood," suggesting in the hieratic image of the sun the possibilities for a redeeming transformation of the natural world.

However, unlike the situation in "A Circle in The Fire," O'Connor does not explicitly force the linkage among the central images in the story and does not arbitrarily resolve the mystery in the action itself. Through a firm control of point of view, she lets the action unfold dramatically so that the girl and the reader are left to make the connections between these images. O'Connor is content to develop the invisible lines which create anagogical motion for both the girl and the reader to intuit. It is left to them to discover the link among the hermaphrodite, the Eucharist, and the "folds of fat" on pig-eared Alonzo's neck. The underlying action of the story is an analogical one, yet O'Connor subtly leads the girl and the reader into a mystery that extends beyond logical deduction and into contemplation.

In "The Life You Save May Be Your Own" O'Connor developed in Mr. Shiftlet a way of seeing reality that is antithetical to the analogical, incarnational perspective and the vision of history it implies. Here, the focusing image is the car which Shiftlet covets. As Hulga does with her wooden leg and Haze Motes does with his car in *Wise Blood,* Shiftlet converts the car into an idolatrous object, a false icon that mirrors his own dualistic sensibility. For him, a true Manichean, spirit is separated from matter. Consequently, his "resurrection" of the defunct automobile is a comically reversed analogical action, a *reincarnation,* since he remakes the car into his own distorted image of reality. For him it is not just a car but the image of his riven self; he sees it as an emblem of disincarnated spirit: "The body, lady, is like a house," he tells Mrs. Crater, "but the spirit is like a car." As a creator of images (and here he resembles a certain kind of artist), Shiftlet, like Hulga, commits the idolatrous act of imposing a transcendent significance on the car and ignoring its concrete reality.[8] To paraphrase O'Connor, Shiftlet's moral sense—the man claims to have "a conscience"— is detached from his dramatic sense; spirit is separated from matter by a typically anti-incarnational vision of the real. Consequently, his flight in the car at the end of the story represents a gnostic attempt to escape incarnate reality, which in his skewed vision Shiftlet sees as only "the rottenness of the world . . . about to engulf him" (*Complete Stories*, p. 156). It is an attempt to transcend history by flight, the reverse of the incarnational movement downward into the concrete to discover its transfiguring possibilities. But his gnostic movement ends in collapse. The car is just a car; it does not satisfy his spirit. His act of "creative" transformation has failed. As an image, the car is not transformed by him into a medium of grace, an object that incarnates the divine. Hence there is no change in his vision of things or their meaning, no revelation of mystery. He is left glumly trapped in his "rotten" world as he races a storm toward Mobile. Against his proclaimed attempts at transcendence, Shiftlet's defeat is the real analogical action of the story, summed up in the "guffawing peal of thunder" that answers his self-pitying cry against a "rotten" world.

Given the complex problem of image-making O'Connor posed for herself—finding images that would function anagogically in a story—it is easy to understand her opinion that "The Artificial Nigger" was perhaps her most successful story. In the statue of the artificial nigger she embodied the extensions of action and meaning as complexly and successfully as she ever had in a single image.

The statue of the artificial nigger, I would argue, best realizes all the anagogical potentialities for the image. Its value as an image is clearly focused upon the consciousness of a character, Mr. Head, and serves to transform that consciousness by a stunning revelation of the meaning of experience. Through the statue, Mr. Head discovers not only the meaning of his present actions but also the ultimate significance of those actions within the cosmic framework of redemption. In early stories such as "A Good Man Is Hard to Find," "The Displaced Person," "A Circle In The Fire," "A Temple of the Holy Ghost," and "Good Country People," the impact of the anagogical image upon the consciousness of protagonists had characteristically been left implicit. In "The Artificial Nigger," the image's anagogical force is explicitly manifested through Mr. Head's radical change of vision. In this story O'Connor managed to solve the artistic problem of the relationship between concrete image and the sin of rebellion which is "of the mind"—a problem she had broached with only partial success in "The Turkey"—and at the same time transform that mind through the grace embodied in the image.

On one level the artificial nigger statue, with its "wild look of misery," embodies an immediate historical reality: the whole history of the sin of racial prejudice adumbrated in the attitudes of Nelson and Mr. Head. But on another level, that immediate historical reality is transfigured into a larger, anagogical context of meaning: the eternal action of man's fall through pride which reaches back to the original rebellion against God. Nelson and Mr. Head stand "gazing at the artificial Negro as if they were faced with some great mystery, some monument to another's victory that brought them together in their common defeat" (*Complete Stories*, p. 269). The image is not static; it dramatically triggers the reconciliation between Mr. Head and Nelson. This mysterious action of grace brings with it a transformed way of seeing. Mr. Head now sees their true link with fallen yet redeemed mankind, symbolized by the statue (like the Grandmother's discovery of her link with fallen humanity in the Misfit), and in seeing this he achieves a true vision of himself. Finally, as an anagogical image the statue also creates a transfigured vision of history, for at the end Mr. Head recognizes his present condition in terms of a context that embraces all time, all history, and the eternal:

> Mr. Head stood very still and felt the action of mercy touch him again but this time he knew that there were no words in the world that could name it. He understood that it grew out of agony, which is not denied to any man and which is given in strange ways to children. He understood it was all a man could carry into death to give his Maker and he suddenly burned with shame that he had so little of it to take with him. He stood appalled, judging himself with the thoroughness of God, while the action of mercy covered his pride like a flame and consumed it. He had never thought himself a great sinner before but he saw now that his true depravity had been hidden from him lest it cause him despair. He realized that he was forgiven for sins from the beginning of time, when he had conceived in his own heart the sin of Adam, until the present, when he had denied poor Nelson. He saw that no sin was too monstrous for him to claim as his own, and since God loved in proportion as He forgave, he felt ready at that instant to enter Paradise. (*Complete Stories*, pp. 269–70)

In the statue of the artificial nigger O'Conner had discovered an image of sufficient power, depth, and mystery to incarnate fully her anagogical vision of reality and history.

Chapter Three
Wise Blood: The Rain of History

O'Connor's first novel, *Wise Blood* (1952), has probably occasioned more critical controversy than any of her other major works. Ten years after its publication, she claimed it was written by "an author congenitally innocent of theory, but one with certain preoccupations," the major ones undoubtedly being a concern with the process of Christian redemption and the mystery of freedom.[1] Yet the novel's angular comic vision, its bizarre yoking of the religious and the grotesque, and its seemingly harsh vision of the world have provoked divided critical reactions which often call into question the essential meaning of the book.[2] Some readers see *Wise Blood* as embodying a Manichean vision of the world and impute this perspective to O'Connor's own subversive imagination. To them, the novel's action, particularly Haze's final self-blinding and death, reveals O'Connor's contempt not only for irreligious modern society but also for physical creation itself, matter and the world of the flesh. Against this view stands O'Connor's claim for the book's orthodox theological vision, albeit invertedly presented. To impute a simple Manichean vision to O'Connor in *Wise Blood*, however, seems to beg the question of the book's complex dimensions. In its totality *Wise Blood* does not, I believe, argue for a Manichean view of reality; but this is not to say that the Manichean view is not a central issue in the novel. Nor is it to say that O'Connor was wholly successful in realizing her "preoccupations." The issue, I would argue, is both literary and theological, and therefore indivisible. The difficulties O'Connor encountered in writing *Wise Blood,* as I hope to show, involve artistic problems in the relationship between image-making and vision, specifically between analogy and comedy, problems not unexpected for a young writer "congenitally innocent of theory."

Wise Blood is about Haze Motes's relationship to history and thus about historical vision. Viewed from the standpoint of O'Connor as artist, the novel concerns the problem of how to make the Christian historical vision manifest in the present irreligious world, how to incarnate it. Again, the issue is rooted in the Incarnation, for the key question Haze asks is about the way in which redemption can be actualized in the present: "where in your time and your body has Jesus redeemed you?" (*Three by Flannery O'Connor*, p. 90). As a question about analogy, it can be rephrased: what is the concrete link between the historical Christ and the present, the world's body? It is a question that was both theologically and artistically decisive for O'Connor, and *Wise Blood* can be viewed reflexively as her attempt to work out her own vision of history in fiction.[3] As such, discussion of this novel might logically precede discussion of the major stories in her first collection, since by and large the problems of image-making in relation to historical vision are more successfully handled in those stories. However, viewing *Wise Blood* in the retrospect of those stories helps clarify the difficulties she faced in the longer narrative, particularly because those difficulties go directly to the heart of the metaphysics of comedy in all her work.

A central problem with *Wise Blood* is the apparent discordance between the concrete images that make up the world of the novel and the historical vision O'Connor wished to convey in the story of Hazel Motes. On the one hand, many of the images create the picture of a harsh world almost totally without capacity for redemption. On the other hand, though her fictional strategy is oblique, O'Connor clearly intends Haze's quest to represent a type of redemption linked directly to the historical Christ whom he is unable to escape. Given this apparent discordance, the novel seems to be at odds with itself—full of exuberant energy and humor but not fully integrated in its total vision. At issue is a question of artistic "balance," one which involves the whole question of the analogical in relation to comic technique. O'Connor formulated the problem in a well-known statement in "The Grotesque in Southern Fiction":

> I am told that the model of balance for the novelist should be Dante, who divided his territory up pretty evenly between hell, purgatory, and paradise. There can be no objection to this, but there also can be no reason to assume that the result of doing it in these times will give us the balanced picture that it gave in Dante's. Dante lived in the thirteenth century, when that balance was achieved in the faith of his age. We live in an age now which doubts both fact and value, which is swept this way and that by momentary convictions. Instead of reflecting a balance from the world around him, the novelist now has to achieve one from a felt balance inside himself. (*Mystery and Manners*, p. 49)

Dante's vision and method were of course analogical. So was O'Connor's; but because O'Connor saw her age as neither Christian nor particularly religious, she claimed the need to distort the literal surface and use the grotesque in order to achieve that "felt balance" as artist. This necessary turning inward to achieve a "felt balance" of faith and vision is in some important respects analogous to Haze Motes's turning within himself to make a personal demonstration of his belief at the end of *Wise Blood*. More immediately, however, the problem of locating balance in fictional vision points to the larger issue of the metaphysics of the grotesque and what relation it bears to the harsh, often repugnant surface of *Wise Blood*.

Behind O'Connor's theoretical justification for the use of the grotesque lies the Christian application of the doctrine of analogy, wherein any image can potentially be an image of redeemed creation. Such an image would be transformable, capable of embodying the action of grace, like the artificial nigger statue or the water stain in "The Enduring Chill." As I have already suggested, O'Connor saw her special problem as a writer to be rooted in the fact that the age speciously believed in its own capacity for achieving wholeness exclusive of the divine, a situation she found truly grotesque. To counteract this belief, she employed distortion to pulverize the specious belief of the age and open her audience to the possibility of the numinous reality beyond the natural world. Using this strategy, she might reveal the anagogical through the literal; she might create a truer image of man as fallen but also full of potential for spiritual transformation through grace.

O'Connor was not unaware of the dangers in this strategy of the grotesque. Frequently she remarked that the problem for the artist who used distortion was to know how to distort without destroying the work. William Lynch sees this as the central problem for the comic artist: "One of the great technical (and theological!) questions, therefore is: How far can you go in inventing interstices and smells for man before you are lodged in the disgusting, the monstrous, and (and this is the point) the non-human? This is the critical problem of the distance between laughter at the human and the non-human" (*Christ and Apollo,* p. 110). Lynch sees the root of the problem as theological, not only because it concerns the fundamental question of the image of man but also because in this analogical view comedy is ultimately grounded in Christ's Incarnation. For him, the essential drive of all comedy is to return man to his truly *human* selfhood and to affirm all his free capacities as a human creature. Comedy, therefore, "is not at all anarchic; it is only a defender of another and more human order (more muddy, more actual, more free). Metaphysically, it is a defender of being against the pure concept or category" (p. 114). Moreover, because comedy recalls man to his true state as human—limited and specific, yet free and potentially divine—it is implicitly rooted in the concrete person of Christ, the defining point of man as human/divine. As a truly comic figure, man is made in the image of Christ. What links this comic vision to Christ, for Lynch, is the doctrine of analogy:

> The medieval idea of the analogy of being is a fascinating doctrine. On the surface all it says is that being is the same and one everywhere, but everywhere profoundly different. Every difference this tremendous drive in the world creates is being and is one. Thus this unity cannot proceed one generative step without creating difference (the many) and without creating itself. Therefore, it need not move out of itself to be enormously creative, open and free. But this is the most fundamental statement of comic remembrance: that a thing need not step out of the human to be all things, and to achieve the liberty of the children of God. The mud in man, the lowermost point in the subway, is nothing to be ashamed of. It can produce (St. Thomas would call it *potentia oboedientialis*) the face of God.
>
> What is funny? Things are funny, precisely because they can recall the relation between God and themselves. (p. 115)

Lynch goes on to point out that one of the typical strategies of comic remembrance is the artist's use of foreshortening, a strategy implicit in the analogical principle: "By foreshortening: the comic is sudden, and full of surprises and skippings of the intervening steps; the man of dignity (he could be the saint) slips on the banana peel. The lion is Bottom. The Pope is dust. Let us not talk of incongruity as the secret clue to comedy, but of congruity, of the tie between the earth and Christ, with all the logic omitted. Why should we laugh or magnify the Lord? Because this is the way things are."[4] Much of the criticism of *Wise Blood* for its so-called harsh view of man, it seems to me, is based upon a sentimental refusal to see "the way things are." What is attributed to O'Connor as distortion in the novel, the product of subversive imagination, is in fact literally realistic and verifiable. As she once noted, there is nothing harder (or more comic, we might add) than Christian realism.

Lynch notes, however, that there are also forms of the pseudocomic, particularly those portraying man as a trapped victim—unfree—or as contemptible and subhuman. The critical question regarding *Wise Blood,* then, is whether O'Connor's comic use of the grotesque is developed in sufficient depth and complexity to convey the truly human image of man as analogically linked to Christ. Does she create the "felt balance" between image and vision she was striving for? In this sense Haze Motes's drama enacts O'Connor's own struggle over this precise artistic and theological issue, and from it I think she learned much about the nature and capacities of her art.

The action of *Wise Blood,* both on the literal and anagogical levels, argues implicitly for a redemptive vision of history, but O'Connor chose to present Haze's quest obliquely as a *via negativa.* This obliqueness made representation of the Christian viewpoint difficult when placed against the array of harsh images that seemingly undercut it. Nevertheless, Haze's quest is essentially about the meaning of the self in history. His early claims to nihilism and innocence are an attempt to escape history, the legacy of original sin transmitted to him as a human being and specified in the guilt he feels over the carnival sideshow visit. There is an implicit question raised by his situation: what does this condition of guilt mean for humanity and how can it be meliorated? To Haze's mother and his preacher uncle it means the inborn condition of sin, only meliorated by Christ's redemption, but Haze spends much of the novel trying unsuccessfully to repudiate this vision of history and at the same time maintain a commitment to absolute truth. Haze's initial attempt to deny personal sinfulness is to claim innocence through a belief in "nothing," but his own sense of truth ironically undermines this position at every turn. Even the concepts of innocence or "bastard" (in Sabbath Lily's case) imply the existence of their opposites, and Haze must either admit an authentic standard of truth or fall into a solipsism that negates the very meaning of his existence. Trapped in his own inconsistencies, Haze then claims the power of self-redemption in his Church Without Christ, an explicit rejection of Christ's redemptive act. Like the Misfit, but without the Misfit's underlying self-pity, Haze disavows "any he'p" for salvation. Thus for him the power of salvation must be totally contained within the self, cut off from history. This situation seems to leave him rootless, divorced from the past yet capable of sustaining an identity in a kind of purely existential, gnostic present; the claim to a purely "present" self is one of the prevalent forms of the gnostic impulse. Therefore his Church Without Christ needs no "set place" to exist, Haze maintains, because it is not linked to any concrete historical order. It is movable, like his car, both of which are metaphors in Haze's view for the spirit's ahistorical encapsulation in the present:

> "Nothing outside you can give you any place," he said. . . . "You can't go neither forwards nor backwards into your daddy's time nor

your children's if you got them. In yourself right now is all the   ·
place you've got. If there was any Fall, look there, if there was any
Redemption, look there, and if you expect any Judgment, look
there, because they all three will have to be in your time and your
body and where in your time and your body can they be?" (*Three by
Flannery O'Connor,* p. 90)

Ostensibly a denial of historical connection, Haze's statement does contain
an ironic truth—the need for commitment to belief in the present—
which will prove his undoing, for the logic of his argument will lead
finally to penitential acts with his own body when his ahistorical quest
fails.

Haze's attempts to escape history are ironically confounded not only by
his own integrity of conscience but also by the world outside himself,
which everywhere mirrors the condition of sin—brokenness, deceit, and
indifference to truth characteristic of the social milieu of the novel. Objects and persons constantly reflect a fallen condition. The ingrained vision of sin and redemption inherited from his mother is specified in her
Bible and glasses which he carries with him, the latter particularly crucial
as an image of seeing when Haze dons the glasses just before he destroys
the "new jesus." The legacy of sin/redemption is echoed in the "ragged
shadow" of Jesus that stalks him from the treeline, in the sour phrases of
the car dealer Slade's son ("Christ nailed"), and in the many road signs
announcing Final Judgment that Haze encounters. More important is the
guilt-ridden Asa Hawks, who in spite of his own failure of faith nevertheless sees Haze's real obsession with Jesus, and his corrupt daughter
Sabbath Lily, who traps Haze because he speciously believes in innocence.
In addition, his rival Onnie Jay Holy's "Church of Christ Without Christ"
is a theological mirror image of Haze's own church, since Holy's doctrine
is a gnostic reconstruction of Christianity based on what the individual
self wants to make of the meaning of its existence in history. His doctrine
of human nature founded in "natural sweetness" (innocence) rejects the
historical fallen condition as thoroughly as Haze does in his rantings,
though Holy's doctrine is more palatable to the unbelieving audience because it offers them the husk of religion without either substance or need
for commitment. Yet even Haze's destruction of this alter-image, which
he regards as an embodiment of false conscience, turns into a *momento
Christi* when the dying Solace Layfield confesses and recognizes the
Redeemer.

Finally, Haze's attempted flight from history is literally undermined by
the repeated breakdowns of the Essex—his vehicle for gnostic escape—

and culminates in its destruction. Once the car is destroyed, Haze turns inward to act out his own integrity and commitment to personal truth by mortification of the body. Although the manner of penance is extreme, the choice behind it is of the utmost importance, because Haze's acknowledgement that he is "not clean" implies an altered vision of history. Instead of claiming autonomous moral self-sufficiency, Haze now recognizes that he has "to pay" for his acts; this realization implies his acceptance of an identity within a spiritual order that extends beyond the self, an identity to which he is accountable. Thus he is linked to man's fallen history. The fact that his admission of sinfulness is not balanced by an explicit vision of the possibilities of redemption *in the world* does not negate the underlying meaning—the analogical action—of his progress and final stance in the novel. However, Haze's situation at the end, in which he is committed to a personal religious vision in an essentially hostile or indifferent world (personified mainly by Mrs. Flood), does suggest much about O'Connor's own predicament as a writer and about the specific problems of transmitting vision in this novel. A clearer way to see this predicament is to examine her method of image-making in *Wise Blood,* particularly in comparison to the major early short stories and to *The Violent Bear It Away.*

The preponderance of mechanistic and animalistic images in *Wise Blood* has been a point of much critical discussion. In writing about this *"Christian malgré lui,"* O'Connor deliberately employed a strategy of flattening the human to the two-dimensional scale of the natural and the artificial. We think immediately of offensive descriptions and behavior, of the many characters described in terms of ugly birds and beasts, and of course of the whole subtheme of Enoch Emery's devolution into an "ape." Much of this strategy undoubtedly stems from O'Connor's penchant for cartooning, her talent for creating stylized humor with a few deft strokes. Certainly *Wise Blood* represents the most extreme example of this penchant. But the more important purpose of such a strategy is to develop the theme of a world that has largely abandoned any interest in the divine and lacks any religious self-image. Since it has largely closed itself to a vision of the transforming power of the numinous, its dominant images reflect that reduction to the natural order which is a logical result of its view of reality. This situation is summed up in the famous opening of chapter 3, one of the few direct references to the transcendent in the book: "The black sky was underpinned with long silver streaks that looked like scaffolding and depth on depth behind it were thousands of stars that all seemed to be moving very slowly as if they were about some vast construction work that involved the whole order of the universe and would take all time to complete."[5] Lacking a vision of the numinous, Haze's world suffers from the kind of metaphysical misplacement that results in idol-making, the worship of an object or image to which a confusion of vision has erroneously imputed transcendent significance. Initially there is the mechanical peeler, hawked as an instrument of magical power by a salesman behind an "altar" table. But this is soon supplanted by the two central images of idolatry: Haze's rat-colored Essex and the new jesus mummy.

Like Mr. Shiftlet, Haze attempts to make an idol of his dilapidated car, a symbol of the gnostic spirit of his quest. In *Wise Blood*, however, the car serves much more forcefully as the focal point of contending visions of history. As a spiritual questor, Haze is torn between his rejection of a purely mechanistic view of things—the redemptive vision of history represented by his mother—and his own inner sense of the spiritual and of freedom to act. Consequently he attempts to escape by creating his own autonomous world signified by the Essex, his "place to be." But to attempt to transfigure the car into a "place to be," a source and locus of being, is to invest it falsely with a spiritual meaning that is metaphysically (and comically we should say, recalling Lynch) at odds with its reality. Like Shiftlet, Haze tries to reincarnate the object by an act of gnosis (the reverse of authentic analogical movement), an act that likewise mirrors his attempt to escape history. But the car fails of such easy transformation. Haze's initial trial drive in the country is comically subverted when rain leaks in all over him; this fiasco is followed by repeated breakdowns of the Essex and of course its eventual destruction, the final straw that leads to Haze's acceptance of his sinful condition.

A similar process of idolization occurs in the case of the new jesus mummy, performed this time by Enoch Emery and Sabbath Lily. Enoch stupidly mistakes Haze's call for a "new man," an ironic inversion of St. Paul's call for spiritual man transfigured in Christ, as a desire for a literal object of worship in the form of the mummy. After stealing it, Enoch keeps it in the "tabernacle" under his sink, treating it as a semidivine object. Enoch hopes the mummy will be the means to realize his simpleminded dream of finding friendship in the hostile world, specifically with Haze. Likewise, the corrupt Sabbath Lily idolizes the mummy as a "baby," the perverse offspring of her illicit "marriage" to Haze. But Haze is wise enough to reject this idolatry. To him the "new jesus" concept he has preached is purely metaphorical—only "a way to say something"; he finally smashes the mummy while Sabbath Lily accuses him of being "mean enough to slam a baby against a wall." For understanding the problems O'Connor faced as a writer in *Wise Blood*, it is not insignificant that Haze is unable to incarnate his spiritual longings in a concrete object, except falsely in the car; in the end O'Connor turned to Haze's own body as the image through which to incarnate his spiritual condition.

But the car and the mummy are essentially negative images, emblems of a desacralized world rendered with comic exaggeration. It is thus revealing to compare them with O'Connor's image-making strategy in other major works, when considering the question of a possible discordance between vision, action, and image in *Wise Blood*. The latter work is generally devoid of those transformable images that play so central a role in the analogical action of their stories—the peacock, the wooden leg, the artificial nigger statue, the birdlike water stain, the bull—central because they both embody mystery and undergo transformation through analogy in the course of the story. Instead, in *Wise Blood* we have mainly comic images of dehumanization. The numinous is evoked only on the periphery, in the mysterious shadow that haunts Haze from the trees. (The fact that it is *a shadow* cast by the sun suggests the desacralized condition of this society.) A signal image of the divine throughout O'Connor's fiction is the sun, particularly as a symbol of the transforming power of divine grace within the natural order. But no sun shines in *Wise Blood*. Instead, rain is the oblique symbol of divine presence, descending on Haze at three crucial turning points in the novel: when it leaks into his "place-to-be" car, when he destroys the new jesus mummy, and when he ventures out blind in the rain and is finally found lying in a drainage ditch at the abandoned construction site. Unlike O'Connor's use of the sun image elsewhere, the rain in *Wise Blood* does not strongly suggest revitalization, even though it does precede Haze's conversion; like the shadow image, it is part of the haunting by history that stalks Haze's quest at every turn. And even here the rain image is developed mainly as a natural force; O'Connor only thinly develops its analogical potential as a symbol and negatively at that.

In *Wise Blood,* then, we have an array of images such as the peeler, the mummy, the car, and Haze's hats that indicate a desacralized world, but none undergo the kind of profound symbolic transformation that would help imagistically *dramatize* a redemptive process at work. Thus the novel's main images, I would argue, are not developed with sufficient depth to convey the numinous and the mysterious at the heart of the analogical technique as a means of presenting a redemptive process at work in *both* theological and artistic terms. No spiritual *action* of transformation occurs within these images—no movement of grace—except the negative action of their comic flattening or destruction, as in the case of the Essex. The images are not asked to function in a Christian analogical sense. The burden for suggesting the redemptive process at work rests upon Haze's private integrity and the action of his progress toward a true sense of his identity in fallen history. This progress too is presented obliquely. By contrast, O'Connor more clearly objectified the conflict over opposing views of history through Rayber and the Tarwaters in *The Violent*

Bear It Away. The conflict in *Wise Blood* is both more diffuse and more internalized within Haze, a situation intensified by the narrative distance O'Connor maintains between Haze and the reader, particularly in the last chapter.

The last chapter culminates the blindness/seeing theme, but in *Wise Blood* the theme of vision is not linked to the transforming, or analogical, action of key images as in other major stories. "The Displaced Person," "Revelation," "A Good Man Is Hard To Find," "The Artificial Nigger," and several other stories end with a revelation of the numinous, experienced either directly by a character or vicariously by the reader (or both). No such revelation occurs in *Wise Blood.* Haze's quest ends in a literal blinding and internal revelation, expressed in his admission that he's "not clean." But this revelation has little objective point of contact besides the landlady Mrs. Flood, who is too blinded by materialism herself to see the religious significance of Haze's actions—although she does seem to intuit something of the spiritual that she lacks. Haze himself remains largely silent. Thus while vision and seeing are implicitly linked to a redemptive view of history in the last chapter, the statement of theme must be inferred rather than fully experienced as mystery by the reader; Mrs. Flood is the dominant focal point for the final action, and even she is kept at a comic distance by the narrator. In fact, O'Connor's distanced perspective generally does not allow for direct focus on the development of Haze's consciousness throughout the novel. His consciousness does indeed change, but we observe the change through alterations in his intellectual positions while preaching in his Church Without Christ and in his active responses to a hostile world. Because the narrative distance is maintained, we are not given many glimpses (even ironic) of Haze's *self*-consciousness—the kind we get, for example, in O'Connor's treatment of the Grandmother, Hulga Hopewell, Mr. Head, Mrs. Shortley, or even the child in "A Temple of the Holy Ghost." It is a question not of creating more sympathy for Haze Motes but of creating a locus of vision *within* the story to carry the full mystery of the redemptive process at work.

In the end, Haze turns to his own body to answer the question he initially raised: "where in your time and your body have you been saved?" The implications of Haze's self-blinding and acts of atonement are crucial and have already been noted: his implicit admission of sinfulness and the need "to pay." Equally important are the implications of this action for O'Connor as writer. Without simplistically identifying her with Haze, we can nevertheless see how the conclusion of *Wise Blood* represents a critical turning point in the development of her analogical method.

After the destruction of the Essex, Haze acknowledges that he is fallen and that there is no escape from the fallen condition. But what can he do next? Where is salvation possible in the present world? "Where in your time and your body have you been saved?" There are almost no signs and no means of salvation in the outer world Haze has experienced. It is a desacralized society given to mechanistic and animalistic standards of behavior, thoroughly dehumanized. Haze's world, the world O'Connor envisioned for him, is not essentially sacramental. Even though at the end Haze becomes one of O'Connor's crypto-Catholics, there are no sacraments in his world, no "outward signs" that can be the media of grace.[6] (The sacraments, of course, are the preeminent example of the analogical principle in theology—the descent of divine grace to transform the physical world.) Lacking these external means of spiritual transformation, Haze necessarily turns inward to act out his belief through his own body. Nevertheless, his acts of penitence are not self-destructive or suicidal attempts to escape the world but the reverse, since after losing the gnostic car his spiritual movement is inward into the fallen physical world of the body. This chosen purgation might be seen as an attempt at self-redemption, especially since he does not explicitly recognize Christ in the last chapters. But it is not like the self-redemption he preached in his Church Without Christ, since he punishes his body now in order to witness explicitly to the integrity of his conscience. Given the desacramentalized character of his world, it is all he can do to demonstrate that integrity as the means of defining his spiritual difference from the world. The alternative would be the dehumanizing "suicide" of capitulation to the natural order represented by Mrs. Flood.

O'Connor's problem as a writer is analogous to Haze's final problem of how to witness to his belief. Like Haze, O'Connor was searching for a "felt balance" of vision. In *Wise Blood* she relied heavily on comic cartooning to express a vision of a world reduced by its own choice to mechanistic and animalistic behavior. She might have continued in this vein as an artist and become essentially a comic satirist only. But she would then have been the artistic equivalent of Haze if he had capitulated sourly to the natural order and become one of its "wise," sardonic citizens without staking his difference in positive terms. O'Connor did not choose this path; in later works she moved beyond comic cartooning either by abandoning it (except for inconsequential characters) or more often by transforming it into something of deeper significance. Still, she did not lose sight of the desacralized world around her.

Another alternative, given this world, might have been for O'Connor to narrow her focus to fictional representation of the relevance of the orthodox sacraments to meaning and action in this desacralized world—their relevance as embodiments of divine mystery. The inclination toward this focus can surely be seen in the importance of the Holy Eucharist in "A Temple of the Holy Ghost" and of course the central action of baptism in *The Violent Bear It Away*. But such an alternative would necessarily have limited her range of fictional vision and made it excessively parochial. She was too conscious of the need to reach an unsympathetic audience to pursue this path exclusively. More important, while such a concentration of emphasis might have been sufficient for the narrow believer as artist, for the artist as believer it would have been antithetical to a vision of the *whole* world as potentially sacramental. In this kind of large vision, *all* the physical reality of the world is capable of being a medium of the action of grace, of freedom, and of mystery—of the redemptive process at work. To incarnate this vision she needed and found the fictional strategy of analogy, a strategy that made it possible to convey all the complex mysteries of vision *through* the image—sun, woods, fire, peacock, bull, water, and bird. With this strategy she moved beyond the limits and problems faced in writing *Wise Blood* to find ways of uniting in single images a vision of creation at once both "full of horror" (evoked by the grotesque) and yet "worth dying for" (redeemable by grace).

Chapter Four
Community in History: Imagining the Mystical Body

When O'Connor talked about the development of her art, she often spoke of "deepening" rather than broadening the mystery. As Robert Fitzgerald pointed out long ago, the vertical image is especially apt given O'Connor's choice to try to perfect her vocation as writer within the given limits of her talent rather than experiment freely with new forms.[1] This vertical image of deepening of course also suggests an analogical movement. O'Connor's choice was as much a matter of remaining true to her vision as to her special talent, true to her vision of the process of history as governed by Christ's Incarnation. Consequently, it is not surprising to find in the stories she wrote from the mid-1950s until her death a pattern of development or deepening that largely involves complexifying and amplifying her essential vision, in terms of both thought and technique. In fact, it is possible to see an analogical relationship between these stories and the earlier *Wise Blood* and *A Good Man Is Hard to Find* collection because she returns again and again to rework and refine the implications of her vision by a process of imaginative transformation. Without pushing the idea too far, one could say that this was part of her own process of redeeming her fictional world, of returning to explore and "link up" different elements of her vision under one comprehensive view of experience governed by mystery. I shall discuss this process in relation to some of the individual stories; the most obvious example is her reworking of "The Geranium," her first story, in "Judgement Day" since the latter is recast precisely in terms of a larger conception of history.

The term *reworking* should not be construed here to mean simply amplification. The question of O'Connor's development is a complex one; it can be understood neither in terms of a sharp demarcation between periods in her career nor in terms of mere amplification of a monolithic orthodox viewpoint. For one thing, her considerable reading in the Bible, theology, philosophy, church history, biography, and psychology had a significant impact upon her thinking. This reading alone deepened her vision of history and what she could make of that vision in fiction without changing the fundamental character of that vision. Still, subtle but telling changes do occur in the stories after 1955. There is less emphasis on the harsh cartoonlike style of characterization and less use of the staged quip or the bizarrely comic action. Notwithstanding obvious exceptions such as Johnson or Singleton, there is also less emphasis upon the extreme figure and the outsider as antagonists. While one may not wish to describe these stories as more mellow, there is certainly less exploitation of the caustic as the dominant tone. Underlying these modifications is a greater emphasis on depicting the process of redemption in relation to the universal social order, the corporate body of the human community moving through history. The different final movements of *Wise Blood* and *The Violent Bear It Away* are a case in point: Haze's retreat from the world contrasts with Young Tarwater's return to the city.

To understand the vision of community in these stories, it is important to recall certain fundamental elements in O'Connor's Christian orthodoxy that shape this vision. Her Catholic belief affirms the existence of a mystical community which is larger than the immediate social community or the "community" that exists between past and present considered in wholly mundane terms. This mystical community is composed of all the living and the dead, who are bonded together by one central act—the Incarnation and Resurrection of Christ, best expressed in St. Paul's definition of the mystical Body of Christ.[2] In this view, history is seen as a dynamic process; it is "being in genesis," to use Tresmontant's phrase, the end of which is fulfillment of this mystical community. The Christian view affirms the process of history to be *collective* and humankind to be a uniquely collective being. The implications of this view are critical in O'Connor's work. Individual refusals of this collective process are manifold, and the dire *cost* of return to this mystical community and collective process is repeatedly dramatized. Moreover, it should be emphasized that for O'Connor this dynamic process of history moving toward fulfillment of the mystical community is the natural state of things, that is, natural in the sense of being consistent with the true nature of man and the true end of being.[3] Therefore death and the other various defects in the world of physical nature are not definitive of the final order of reality.

The philosophical principle underlying this idea of the mystical community is the doctrine of analogy. To say that history is dynamic, that it is "being in genesis" though still unfulfilled, is to say that it is engaged in a process of creation. The source of this process is the source of being itself, God, who communicated being in the original, still-ongoing act of genesis in which all reality continually participates. Creation participates in Divine Being analogically; the principle of analogy is a principle of participation. As Etienne Gilson has explained, analogy explains causality and finality in the universal process.[4] Consequently, man participates in the mystical community by virtue of what he is, his being, and for him to act creatively in this community is to act by cooperative participation in the gradual process of its fulfillment. O'Connor recognized this larger meaning of creativity, rooted in the principle of analogical action, as the particular vocation of the prophetic artist in relation to history and the immediate community. Creativity involves the analogical act of spiritualizing the material; it means creating the immediate and the concrete analogically, that is, in the light of participation in the mystical reality. O'Connor underscored the meaning of this creativity for the artist in her review of Teilhard's *The Phenomenon of Man* and Tresmontant's analysis of Teilhard's work:

> "Humanity," Teilhard wrote, "is very far from being fully created, neither in its individual development nor, above all, in the collective terminus toward which it is directed. . . ." Tresmontant points out that asceticism in Teilhard's view no longer "consists so much in liberating and purifying oneself from 'matter' "—but in further spiritualizing matter . . . in sanctifying and spiritualizing the real which has been given to us, by "working together" with God. Actually Teilhard's work is a scientific rediscovery of St. Paul's thought.
>
> Because Teilhard is both a man of science and a believer, the scientist and the theologian will perhaps require a long time to sift this thought and accept it, but the poet, whose sight is essentially prophetic, will at once recognize in this immense vision his own. Teilhard believed that what the world needs now is a new way to sanctity. His way, that of spiritualizing matter, is actually a very old way, one which throughout history is always being obscured by one form of heresy or another. It is the path which the artist has always taken to his particular goals. (*The Presence of Grace*, pp. 87–88)

It is this larger concept of creativity in relation to the corporate process of realizing the mystical community that should be recalled when discussing O'Connor's frequent use of patterns of sterility and fecundity in her fiction. Natural and symbolic sterility (Julian, Hulga, Asbury, Mrs. May, Mrs. Cope, and so on) are the concrete signs of a spiritual sterility that tries to deny creative participation in the mystical community. In the

Christian view of historical process, to "be creative" is to imitate the source of being by being creative *in His will,* and the special task of the believer-artist in this regard is to witness to this ongoing mystical process in history by imitating in art that analogical process of spiritualizing the material.

O'Connor's belief in this mystical community and the unified corporate process of history is the informing vision in "Greenleaf." Mrs. May's struggle against the Greenleafs and their stray bull is her struggle to resist that dynamic process of growth and to resist her corporal link to it. This historical process is most clearly seen in O'Connor's handling of the European motif in the story, particularly in her transformation of it in terms of a larger universal vision. Comic references to Europe as a place of evil and suffering abound in O'Connor's early fiction.[5] We recall how the Grandmother in her conversation with Red Sammy in "A Good Man is Hard To Find" blames Europe for the ills of the world and how Mrs. Cope's patronizing litanies about European suffering in "A Circle in the Fire" become a personal reality when, her woods ablaze, she takes on the look of misery like the Europeans she imagined. In "The Displaced Person" the European motif occupies center stage, with the Guizacs symbolically representing those who cooperate with the dynamically creative movement of history. In spite of his agonizing history of suffering and displacement, Mr. Guizac is progressive in every way: adept with modern machinery, he is a hard worker who cooperates with every opportunity for advancement. Of course his plan to marry his cousin to a Negro symbolically represents an "ultimate" in social advancement, a plan rooted in the idea of the mystical community of mankind.

In "Greenleaf" O'Connor deepened and transformed the European motif from its earlier depictions more completely. The Greenleaf sons represent an even further "advance" of the corporate process of history. Unlike the rather marginal Guizac family—marginal in relation to the established social order of Mrs. McIntyre's world—the younger Greenleafs are at the center of the process of historical change dramatized in the story. They have benefited by their association with Europe in every way, cooperating with every chance to develop themselves. Service in the war provided them with postwar education and loans to build and modernize their farm; their marriages to French wives literally meld the two cultures and both Greenleaf sons produce thriving families. To Mrs. May this advancement is a horror; she informs her own sons in a shocked voice that soon the Greenleafs will become "Society," her conception of society being of course mundane and secular rather than of any mystical community. This dynamic process of creative action in history is represented concretely (and comically) in the stray Greenleaf bull. In fact, the struggle focuses literally on the question of generation: Mrs. May attempts to keep the bull from upsetting her cows' breeding schedule, and for her the bull comes to embody all the larger forces of generation and change which threaten her control of her confined world. That her world is stagnant is underscored by the contrast between the Greenleaf sons' active participation in the process of historical growth and her own feckless bachelor sons, both sterile bystanders. Equally significant in this regard is the fact that the stray bull is described as a "lover" and a "free spirit" in the story. In the Christian analogical view of history, the initial act of genesis by God is a free act of love, His communication of being. This creative action of love and freedom is the driving force within the redemptive process of history; it is the energy moving history toward fulfillment of the mystical community. Once the bull is seen in this context, the fact that Mrs. May is gored to death by him is incidental to the main fact that in death she, like Mrs. Shortley, is just beginning to learn about her true relationship to the mystical community; she dies in a symbolic act of recognition, "whispering some last discovery into the animal's ear."

But O'Connor's deepening of the European motif in "Greenleaf" is not simply an amplification of theme. Her deepening involves a unification of historical vision and analogical technique in such a way that the story enacts the vision more fully than in either "A Circle in the Fire" or "The Displaced Person." Specifically, O'Connor fuses mythological-pagan and historical-Christian analogues and levels of meaning within individual literal images and actions to create an "identity" between them that not only depends on an analogical technique, but which also reveals the meaning of their complex analogical relationship. For example, on one level the struggle between Mrs. May and the Greenleaf bull specifically evokes various pagan myths of fertility and sacrifice, most notably the Hera-Zeus stories. But such an analogue is ontologically limited in what it can reveal about the range of human experience and the ultimate goal of historical process. Romano Guardini describes this pagan mythical view and its limitations as inherent to man of the classical age:

> From his religious convictions he knew of a "highest father of the gods and men," but this father belonged to his own world just as did the vaults of heaven; in truth he was their very spirit. Classical man knew the power of a Fate which commanded his world; he knew of a governing justice and a reasonable order for all things. These forces, all powerful though they were, did not stand beyond the world but formed within its ultimate order.

Classical man knew nothing of a being existing beyond the
world; as a result he was neither able to view or shape his world
from a vantage point which transcended it. With his feelings and
imagination, in his action and all his endeavors, he lived within his
cosmos. Every project which he undertook, even when he dared to
go to the farthest bounds, ran its course within the arc of his
world. (*The End of the Modern World*, p. 18)

In "Greenleaf," the mythical pagan level of the analogue is fulfilled by
the Christian analogue in which the bull mysteriously signifies lover-vio-
lator-redeemer, an agent in the larger cosmic process of creation. And the
fact that the Christian analogue coexists with the pagan-mythical without
canceling it and within a single image indicates the precise analogical
relationship between the two orders of reality viewed in terms of a historical vision that sees history as driving toward fulfillment of the mystical
community. Put differently, O'Connor is here enacting the relationship
between myth and history through her linking of pagan myth, Europe,
and America under the Christian vision. Hers is a vision of the transforming creative power within history, a vision made concrete by the power of
artistic transformation of specific images and actions within the story. In
"Greenleaf," I would argue, she in effect redeems the many images of
Europe in her stories by linking them together fully within a universal
vision of the historical process.

O'Connor's most direct treatment of this historical process came in "Everything That Rises Must Converge," but here the emphasis is on the
refusal to participate in that process and the terrible costs that refusal
entails. The Teilhardian title specifically evokes the Christian idea of history as an evolutionary movement leading toward final "convergence" in a
mystical community, but O'Connor's adaptation of the theme stresses humanity's capacity for rejecting cooperation with that process and for resist-
ing transformation. Thus the story dramatizes the violent convergence of
different visions of history and the self-inflicted spiritual violence suffered
by those who resist accepting their identity within the corporate unity.

The view of history implicitly held by Julian's mother is retrogressive
and in that respect it is similar to that of her "double" in the story, the
large Negro woman on the bus. Regarding the blacks' drive for social
equality, Julian's mother believes that "they should rise, but on their own
side." Aristocratic and patronizing, her view is based upon her memory of
a childhood in the old hierarchic South which she has romanticized into an
image of order and stability. This view, of course, masks the true source of
her dissociation from history: her underlying prideful belief in her own

superiority separates her from any authentic involvement in the corporate process of change. Though she prides herself on having adapted with dignity to social change, in fact she has resisted true association at every turn.[6]

Her condition is ironically underscored by the key images of transformation in the story—mock transformation, that is—such as the "reduced circumstances" that she and Julian now find themselves in and her attendance in a reducing class at the YMCA, as if transformation were simply a question of physical fitness. The truth, of course, is that she has not essentially changed at all, a fact demonstrated by her spiritual "return" to childhood after being struck by the Negro woman. She regresses to what she has always been, a child linked to the aristocratic Chestneys and Godhighs, as in dying she calls for her grandfather and her maid to take her "home." This regression is appropriate in the sense of being retribution for her presumptuous dissociation from the reality of history; more significantly, it is a return to the only starting point in "childhood" from which any true spiritual growth might possibly begin.

Though based upon a history of discrimination, the Negro woman's attitude is no less retrogressive than Julian's mother's when viewed in terms of the larger vision of a mystical community. Equally proud, she stands ready to resist any movement toward convergence even *before* Julian's mother begins to patronize her child; consequently, her final assault on Julian's mother is but the overt expression of her general spiritual disposition. Given the similarity of attitude in the two women, it is crucially important that the locus of their confrontation should be the black child Carver. As a child, Carver becomes the point of convergence not so much between opposing attitudes of the black and white women as between their mutual regressive views and the vision of mystical community he represents in potentiality. With his playfulness and unsuspicious acceptance of both worlds, he embodies the potential for transformation and progressive convergence suggested by the Christian vision of history. But blinded by pride, neither woman wishes to see him in this capacity. Julian's mother patronizes him in an attempt to fit him into her regressive view, while the child's mother, projecting her own proud isolation onto him, threatens to "knock the living Jesus" out of him if he does not behave.

It is in Julian himself that O'Connor presents the most complex version of the theme of convergence within and with history. His name, the reference to him as looking like a martyr who had "lost his faith," and his mother's repeated defense of his failure to establish a career—"Rome wasn't built in a day"—symbolically link him with Julian the Apostate's defection from and attempt to reverse the spread of Christianity.[7] More-over, this Julian is another of O'Connor's sterile would-be artists, so the theme of commitment to history is given an added dimension by particu-lar reference to the artist's need for "convergence" with the real if he is ever to transform and transfigure it. Such a convergence, of course, would itself be an analogical movement of "descent" into the actuality of history, but Julian is too withdrawn into the inner recesses of his mind to be willing to undertake such action. Throughout much of the story Julian continually withdraws into his mental world where he can enact fantasies of revenge against his mother, invent false bonds of communion with Negroes to prove his liberalism, and pursue flights of nostalgic longing for a patrician identity in the old hierarchic South. The irony is that in his dissociation from reality Julian is just as elitist as his mother, just as proudly isola-tionist in his stance toward the real historical process, though he protests that it is only she who needs to face reality. Julian completely disavows any connection with his mother's world and her thinking, but the action of the story is designed to reveal to him their mutual dependence and similarity.

The fact that much of the story is focused on the conflict between Julian's mental world, governed largely by self-deception, and the objec-tive process of history indicates a further deepening of O'Connor's explora-tion of the relationship between consciousness and history. This topic will be treated more fully in the final chapter, but here we can note how central the theme had become in her fiction.[8] Julian resembles Hulga Hopewell in his entrapment within an enclosed consciousness, but more than in the case of Hulga, Julian's mental dissociation is specifically set against a historical process to which he refuses to commit himself, symbolized in the story by the child Carver. In "Greenleaf" O'Connor presents the his-torical theme involving Mrs. May's conflict with the Greenleafs with more objective narrative distance from the action. In Julian's case the conflict is more internalized, that is, defined in terms of his mind's relationship to the external reality of history. Julian's final "convergence" is not with a bull but with the bitter knowledge of his own capacity for self-deception, his apostasy from history. In his mother's death he is forced to recognize his destructive dependence upon her, and like her, he is symbolically "returned" to the state of childhood, crying "Momma, Momma!" as she collapses. But since Julian has tried to base his whole existence on his self-created fantasies, the revelation is so devastating that his final action be-comes a desperate attempt to resist convergence with history. The last line of the story suggests this: "The tide of darkness seemed to sweep him back to her, postponing from moment to moment his entry into the world of guilt and sorrow." Thus his last move is the reverse of the movement into history we see in Haze Motes and in young Tarwater; but of course Julian's "return" to his mother can be only a temporary postponement. Like Hulga, Julian will live on to confront the demands of the real objective historical process again; in this episode his ironic convergence with history has implicitly brought about a "rising" in his consciousness by a paradoxical destruction of his self-sufficient mental world. Never again will he have his mother's falsely aristocratic stance to depend upon to serve him as the convenient, secure object of his mental ridicule and self-justification. In the story his false spiritual and intellectual haven from history has been destroyed, though of course he is still free to fantasize another escapist haven.

The mysterious role of evil—or potential evil—in the drive of history toward fulfillment of the mystical community is the central theme of "A View of the Woods," a story in which O'Connor again "gathered up" and deepened motifs from earlier works. O'Connor dramatized in the conflict between Mary Fortune Pitts and her grandfather Mr. Fortune two conflicting visions of the corporate process of history. Mr. Fortune's vision is purely mechanistic and secular. His hubristic idea of transforming nature is of something that can be done by a bulldozer, and he attacks any *human* obstacles, represented by the Pitts family, with the same ruthless willpower that he attacks nature. Nothing should stand in the way of his idea of "progress," the most ruthless aspect of which is not so much his transformation of the landscape as it is his satanic attempt to create his granddaughter in his own image—"pure Fortune." Ironically, his notion of progress is as blindly mechanical and truly sterile as the stationary "yellow-monster" seen gorging itself on clay at the beginning and the end of the story.

The contrary vision of history represented by Mary Fortune Pitts and her family suggests the necessary and mysterious role of evil in the process of spiritual transformation. Only by recognition of this fact can truly *human* development occur because it presupposes an accurate vision of what human nature is in all its capacities and limitations. The emphasis on recognizing this essential bond in humanity—the "Pitts" in mankind—is crucial. The story is titled "A View of the Woods," not just "The Woods"; O'Connor again links the central image of the story—the woods—to the act of "seeing" in such a way as to make that image function analogically as a focal point of historical vision.

This technique of transformation can perhaps best be seen by again noting O'Connor's extension of earlier motifs in "A View of the Woods." The image of the construction site, for example, was echoed slightly in "A

Circle in the Fire" in the delinquent boy's remark that if he owned Mrs. Cope's farm he would pave it over for a parking lot and destroy her woods. In that story, the "woods" motif serves mainly as an image of Mrs. Cope's fear and willful desire to control her kingdom; for her the forest serves as a "defense line" against any intruding evil. In *Wise Blood,* the construction site is linked with the larger redemptive process of "construction" at work in the universe and with Haze's spiritual quest, but the image is not emphasized as a major point of revelation. In fact, rather than seeing any deeper significance in the construction site, Haze and the other characters ignore it. The woods in *Wise Blood* and "A Circle in the Fire" also serve as images of mystery, of moral development, and, by extension, of the redemptive process. Again, however, their important symbolic function in these works remains peripheral, especially when we recall that the woods are destroyed at the end of "A Circle in the Fire" and are largely deemphasized in the last chapters of *Wise Blood.*

In "A View of the Woods," the image of construction, now identified with a purely mechanical, secular view of the progress of history, is of central importance in the action of the story. Mary Fortune and the old man watch "the big disemboweled gullet gorge itself on clay," while Mr. Fortune proclaims: "Any fool that would let a cow pasture interfere with progress is not on my books." Similarly, the image of the woods is no longer a static or peripheral motif but is made the focus of an organic, mysterious process of transformation linked explicitly to mystical vision. In the story's opening the trees are described as "a black line of woods which appeared at both ends of the view to walk across the water and continue along the edge of the fields." The reference to walking on water is of course generally Christic, but more significant is the specific biblical analogue of the blind man who, having been cured by Christ, now sees men "as if they were trees, only moving."[9] The blind man has been gifted with mystical vision; he sees the spiritual unity that exists in all creation, sees the spiritual in nature, and sees that man and nature are part of a total dynamic process of genesis, moving toward fulfillment. His is a vision of the true "laws" of nature—the spiritual laws—as O'Connor indicated in her letter to "A" (see note 3). We recall also her use of this reference to the cured blind man's mystical insight as an image of the prophetic artist's vision in her essay "Catholic Novelists and Their Readers."[10] In sum, then, the woods stand as an image of the mysterious possibilities of spiritual transformation in reality and of *seeing* reality precisely in those terms.

Young Mary Fortune's childlike understanding of this vision is evident from her insistence, even to the point of a death struggle with her grandfather, that they not lose "a view" of the woods. Though Mr. Fortune is presented with the opportunity of grasping such a vision, he rejects it completely.

> The third time he got up to look at the woods, it was almost six o'clock and the gaunt trunks appeared to be raised in a pool of red light that gushed from the almost hidden sun setting behind them. The old man stared for some time, as if for a prolonged instant he were caught up out of the rattle of everything that led to the future and were held there in the midst of an uncomfortable mystery that he had not apprehended before. He saw it, in his hallucination, as if someone were wounded behind the woods and the trees were bathed in blood. After a few minutes this unpleasant vision was broken by the presence of Pitt's pick-up truck grinding to a halt below the window. He returned to his bed and shut his eyes and against the closed lids hellish red trunks rose up in a black wood. (*Complete Stories*, p. 348)

Rejecting this true vision is in effect a rejection of the mystical community, and Mr. Fortune is fittingly left abandoned and alone in his dying moments. In his mind he may have destroyed his "future" in assaulting Mary Fortune; he does not see that his blindness had already destroyed his spiritual future in his ruthless attempt to extirpate the "Pitts" from reality. As his heart swells, he runs toward the lake to "escape and leave the woods behind him," but there is no escaping the consequences of his mechanistic vision: "On both sides of him he saw that the gaunt trees had thickened into mysterious dark files that were marching across the water and away into the distance. He looked around desparately for someone to help him but the place was deserted except for one huge yellow monster which sat to the side, as stationary as he was, gorging itself on clay" (*Complete Stories*, p. 356). The fact that the trees are seen here as moving— "marching across the water"—and that both Mr. Fortune and the bull-dozer are seen as "stationary" underscores the true inertness, or the literal materialism, of Mr. Fortune's secular vision juxtaposed against the mystical process incarnated in the image of the marching trees. In her review of Teilhard, O'Connor had talked about the task of "spiritualizing matter" as the poet's way of witnessing to the ongoing redemptive process in creation. This task is precisely what she had accomplished by developing her total "view of the woods"—of nature and man as incomplete but moving toward fulfillment—in this story.

The idea of mystical community, then, presupposes acceptance of the world of nature and the human community, a recognition of the world as it is and of one's place within it. In Julian's case this recognition—a necessary descent from his rarefied intellectual "bubble" into the reality of history—awaits him after the death of his mother. Only through such recognition and acceptance can the true work of progress occur, a process of transformation empowered by the divine spirit and man's cooperation with it. This necessary descent into history is a movement O'Connor delineated even more fully in the case of Asbury Fox in "The Enduring Chill."

Asbury's condition resembles Julian's in that they both have retreated from reality through false transcendence into a gnostic mental world. Asbury's condition also resembles that of Hulga and the Misfit in that all three attempt self-creation of an identity (Hulga and the Misfit's renaming indicates this) which is in fact idolatrous. The transcendent identities they try to claim for themselves in truth represent acts of disincarnation, their attempted apostasy from the corporate bond of humankind. Asbury's specific idols are art and the image of himself as a would-be artist; he attempts unsuccessfully to achieve a transformation of himself by his own power and a transformation of reality through art. What is new in "The Enduring Chill" is the manner in which O'Connor deepened the theme of the necessary descent into history by focusing it explicitly in terms of the concept of spiritual transformation within the mystical body. Behind Asbury's condition both as man and would-be artist, illuminating it at every turn, is the Pauline theme of the mystery of the "spiritual body," the transformation of man and nature into the "New Man" and new creation. Doctrinally, this transformation is the final goal in the historical process of "spiritualizing matter" made possible by Christ's Incarnation and Resurrection. In "The Enduring Chill" O'Connor specifies this theme of spiritual transformation in terms of the function of art and the artist and thereby incorporates her vision of art within the larger vision of the mystical body.

On the widest level of action, then, "The Enduring Chill" centers on a movement of incarnation and incorporation; Asbury's descent into the world's body is the only means through which spiritual transformation can occur. Given Asbury's pretensions, in one sense the action is ironic, but on a deeper level the action recapitulates the Christian paradox of analogy: the way to transfiguration is through descent—into the body, into history, and into death—in imitation of Christ's redemptive act. Asbury initially sees himself as above the natural and human world around him. Having reluctantly returned home from New York only to "die," he despises his sister Mary George and is revulsed by his mother's commonsense solicitude for his health; he regards both as too stupid to understand his exalted temperament. Likewise, he believes his ailment is "way beyond" the bumptious Dr. Block, and he is mortified on his return to the farm when one of the cows stares at him as if there were some mysterious bond between them. This shock of recognition conveys an ironic truth: Asbury's unavoidable link with the physical world of nature is underscored by the fact that his illness, undulant fever like "Bangs in a cow," is due to drinking contaminated milk.

Asbury's spiritual progress in the story, then, involves a necessary return to the concrete, a recognition of his link with the natural and human orders and his own spiritual as well as artistic sterility. Even his most elaborate would-be "creative" act in the story—his death and the preparations for it—is conceived in falsely transcendent terms and is comically undercut at every turn. His dream of a stately funeral ends with a vision of a cow licking his head; his staged leave-taking with the Negroes Morgan and Randall—a false attempt to create spiritual community—turns into farce; his hoped-for "communion" with an intellectual Jesuit becomes a brusque harrowing of his spiritual pride; and finally Asbury scrambles to recover the self-pitying, Kafka-esque letter—his one literary product—that he has written condemning his mother for his own failures. All his efforts at false transcendence are defeated, and he is finally left with the unspectacular knowledge of his own limited humanity, that he would live "for the rest of his days, frail, racked, but enduring . . . [yet] in the fact of a purifying terror" (*Complete Stories,* p. 382). This revelation purifies his mind because Asbury, shredded of illusions, knows the truth of his place in the world; the revelation brings "terror" because he must live in the face of this glimpsed absolute knowledge of himself. The question he faces now is not so much the Eliotic one: "After such knowledge, what forgiveness?"; rather, it is the more radically Christian one: what do I make of my world in the light of this truth I have been given? His progress, then, has followed the lines of analogical movement, and in the end he ironically becomes a "new man" by virtue of this gift of insight into his true condition brought about by the descent of the icy Paraclete.

On another level, as I have mentioned, "The Enduring Chill" develops the theme of spiritual transformation in terms of the artist's function within the mystical community. As a would-be artist Asbury is sterile, a condition due in part both to his dissociation from the corporate world and to the fact that he has made art his god—an idol to worship. To art he has attributed the power of salvation through human effort alone, a power invested in human imagination capable of transforming reality and the self. Asbury's view is suggestively similar to that expressed by Stephen Daedalus, whose concept of the epiphany in *A Portrait of the Artist as a Young Man* implies that the artist can create the world in his own image, transfigure it solely by human imagination, and thereby become godlike in his creative actions. The fact that Stephen's theory represents a perversion of Aquinian ontology and metaphysics, as a number of scholars have noted, is extremely important here because Stephen's theory shifts the source of the analogical view of reality from Being itself to the creative faculty of the artist and thus radically alters the entire view of reality and the artist's relationship to it.[11] In Stephen's view, the godlike artist makes analogy according to his own lights, rather than discovering the ultimate reaches of mystical community through analogy. The latter is the role of the prophetic artist, and it is this idea that O'Connor implicitly sets against Asbury's idea of the artist as independent godlike creator. The prophetic artist is a participant in the corporate process of redemption history, a "seer" of the meaning of things near at hand in the light of their ultimate destiny. Thus his visionary power is rooted in the action of creative transformation sustained in history not solely by independent human imagination but by the Holy Spirit and human cooperation with it. This prophetic vision of creation, including artistic creation, is the deeper implication in Father Vogle's remark to Asbury that there is "a real probability of the New-Man, assisted, of course, . . . by the Third Person of the Trinity" (*Complete Stories*, p. 360). As a would-be artist Asbury identified his whole self with the role of writer; the devastating failure of his talent thus represents for him a threatening collapse of his being. His self-constructed, transcendent kingdom of art is an idolatrous one which he has set up in opposition to the larger, truer world of history and the mystical community. Consequently, in the final descent of the Holy Spirit, Asbury is given a true epiphany of who he is in relation to this community and is himself ironically but creatively transformed into the "New Man" with a truer, more prophetic vision of his condition and his future.

O'Connor's concern with the theme of the idolatrous self, the idolatrous view of art as a means of salvation, coupled with the theme of the necessary descent into history, is deepened further in "Parker's Back." Like Asbury, Parker would choose the art object—in this case tattoos—as a substitute means of salvation. He claims that there is "nothing in particular to save himself from"; nevertheless, his spirit is dissatisfied, and he chooses tattooing as his means of self-redemption because it will transform him from an ordinary youth into a unique individual, above the common lot of humanity. In effect, Parker tries to make himself into an idol of self-worship; his tattooing is designed both to fulfill his pride and to seduce women. The pattern is a familiar one in O'Connor's fiction. Parker echoes Haze Motes in his denial of the need for salvation; like Haze, the critical events in his apostasy are a visit to a carnival, where he first sees tattoos, and his career in the service, where his dissolute life flourishes. In terms of representing a presumed moral self-sufficiency, Parker's tattooing is analogous to Haze's created idol—the Church of Christ Without Christ—with the crucial difference that Haze is more intelligent and does not identify the thing with what it signifies; Haze believes his new church is "just a way to say something." Parker also resembles Hulga and the Misfit in that his apostasy involves naming as part of the process of attempted self-redemption by "claiming a difference" and denying one's true being. Parker would reject his given biblical names Obadiah Elihue as part of his idolatrous self-transformation.

Parker's rejection of the Old Testament names, coupled with his false transcendence through idolization, clearly denotes his attempt to deny his place in salvation history, an attempt specified in his relationship with his wife Sarah Ruth. She is explicitly linked to this salvation history by her own biblical names, by her rejection of his tattoos, and by the fact that she directly invokes the mystical community by reminding Parker that he will have to answer for his actions at the Last Judgment. Parker, on the other hand, says he has no use for "long views." Still, the fact that he is mysteriously attracted to Sarah Ruth in spite of himself indicates his potential for real spiritual growth, and it is this potential to which Sarah Ruth responds and not his flagrantly decorated body.

Nevertheless, Parker would subdue her, would "bring her to heel," with his idolatrous use of art in trying to win her approval with a tattoo of the Byzantine Christ. On one level, his use of the tattoo is idolatrous because as a means of self-worship it would enable him to deny his real historical identity and also to seduce his wife to such a vision. On another level, it is idolatrous because in using the tattoo, Parker ironically identifies the object with that which it signifies, as he does when he tries to use the tattoo of the Byzantine Christ to subdue Sarah Ruth and calls the picture "God." But she is not to be seduced into a vision she sees as blatantly idolatrous. Sarah Ruth's religious fundamentalism has its comic value in the story (she regards a church as idolatrous and refuses to be married in one), but this humor should not obscure the more important fact that she does not confuse the sign with the reality. When she rejects the Byzantine Christ tattoo she proclaims that God is a "spirit"; she does not identify the reality of God with a pictorial representation, as Parker's seductive attempt to "bring her to heel" would. Similarly, she does not identify Parker's spirit exclusively with his tattooed body; in rejecting his tattooing as idolatrous she is able to see the egotistic yet potentially redeemable spirit underlying his actions. When she forces him to use his true biblical name, Obadiah, his acceptance of this identity immediately effects a transformation in his spirit that is manifested through the body: " 'Obadiah,' he whispered and all at once he felt the light pouring through him, turning his spider web soul into a perfect arabesque of colors, a garden of trees and birds and beasts" (*Complete Stories,* p. 528). Her insistence that he accept his true name, then, effects an integration of body and spirit.

I think it is a mistake to see Sarah Ruth's rejection of the tattoos and her thrashing of Parker simplistically as evidence of her Manichean denial of the physical. The point is much more important. Sarah Ruth is involved in the corporate body by virtue of her marriage to Parker and, more significantly, by her pregnancy. As her biblical name suggests, her marriage and childbearing are to be seen as her involvement in the process of redemption in history; she effects symbolically the transformation of the whole person by insisting that Parker use his own biblical name. Thus when she subdues him with a broom until welts appear on the Byzantine tattoo, she is chastizing his errant spirit to return him to who he truly is. That chastizement is based upon a love of what Parker truly is and truly can be. This hard, demanding love is the spirit behind his transformation; the same demanding love is the driving force of redemption in history, centered in Christ.[12] "Parker's Back" is unique in O'Connor's canon because its theme of love is focused directly in terms of a vital man-woman relationship governed by the "long view" of mankind's place and role in the mystical community.

The long view of history, the process which for O'Connor culminates in the resurrection of the body and final judgment, was the dimension she added when she fleshed out her first published story "The Geranium" into "Judgement Day." Like "A View of the Woods," the story also dramatizes two conflicting visions of history and progress, two ideas of change here particularly embodied in the relationship between whites and Negroes, as in "Everything That Rises Must Converge." The New York world of Tanner's daughter is one ostensibly marked by social progress, at least to the extent that a relative equality exists between whites and Negroes. But underlying this superficial advance is the deeper fact of spiritual alienation, signified by the estrangement from others that characterizes urban life there, the people of each race guardedly "minding their own business." In short, it is a mock community, a perversion of the idea of mystical community, a society which has lost the long view of history because it has turned away from the spiritual roots of such a mystical vision. Tanner's daughter tells him that his ideas of death, judgment, heaven, and hell are "a lot of hardshell Baptist hooey"; similarly, when he calls the Negro actor "preacher," the actor screams "I'm not even no Christian. I don't believe that crap. There ain't no Jesus and there ain't no God" (*Complete Stories*, p. 545). Having abandoned a vision of the ultimate reaches of human community, this society's so-called "tolerance" becomes a secular parody of the idea of the corporate unity of mankind and the movement toward fulfillment. For Tanner's daughter and the Negro actor, fulfillment means self-satisfaction in purely mundane terms, and the process ceases with death.

Tanner's own spiritual failings are manifest in the story and are not extenuated. A prideful sense of racial superiority has led him to "control" Coleman for years, and his proud refusal to work for the part-Negro Dr. Foley is directly responsible for his present predicament in New York. He has since come to recognize his folly: "If he had known it was a question of this—sitting here looking out of this window all day in this no-place, or just running a still for a nigger, he would have run the still for the nigger. He would have been a nigger's white nigger any day" (*Complete Stories*, p. 540). It is because of this folly and his general prejudice that he must undergo a violent "judgment day" at the hands of the Negro actor in their last encounter on the stairway. But this secular judgment is secondary and incidental when compared to the final judgment he must undergo before God, just as the fact of his death is secondary to the larger question of his ultimate spiritual destiny.

In spite of his moral failings, Tanner has not lost sight of the long view of history, extending to the final Resurrection. Prejudiced on the one hand, Tanner has also genuinely cared for Coleman, and his concern is the mark of a true *human* bond of community, albeit flawed, against which the alienation and indifference of the New York "tolerant" world is to be measured. Having intuited the spiritual rootlessness of a world that has abandoned any sense of its ultimate direction, he warns Coleman that New York is "no kind of place." At the same time, Tanner never loses sight of his ultimate destiny. He dies struggling to return "home" to that world still possessed of a sense of mystical community. Equally important, he dies possessed of a vision of history that includes trust in the Lord and a vision of his own bodily resurrection on judgment day. As he begins his final journey Tanner recites the twenty-third Psalm ("The Lord is my shepherd . . . I shall not want"), and his dreamed arrival in Georgia prefigures his resurrection: "In a moment a shaft of greenish light fell on him. He pushed through it and cried in a weak voice: 'Judgement Day! Judgement Day! You idiots didn't know it was Judgement Day, did you?'" (*Complete Stories*, p. 549).

The same vision of mystical community which underpins "Judgement Day" is rendered even more explicitly in "Revelation," a story which in many ways best demonstrates how O'Connor gathered up the themes of her work processively and deepened them through analogical technique. In "Revelation," the idea of mystical community is developed precisely in terms of a vision of history that unites Old Testament and New Testament analogues and is made concrete in the hierophany Mrs. Turpin has about her place in that community near the end of the story. Mrs. Turpin is the last in a long line of arrogant self-righteous farm women that stretches from Mrs. Crater and Mrs. Cope to Mrs. Shortley and Mrs. McIntyre and to Mrs. May in "Greenleaf." However, O'Connor's treatment of Mrs. Turpin is different and more sympathetic in the sense that she is not destroyed or completely devastated in the process of illumination as many of the other women are; here O'Connor chose instead to render the dutiful, morally smug farm woman in the light of a charitable vision that affords Mrs. Turpin her due place in the redemptive process. In this sense, her final vision of the souls marching to heaven, herself included, is an "answer," within O'Connor's canon, to Mrs. Shortley's self-righteous vision of herself as a prophetess and avenging angel of God in "The Displaced Person."

The crucial difference in the treatment of Mrs. Turpin centers upon her acceptance, albeit painfully, of the grace offered which enables her to see her true place in the mystical community; O'Connor explicitly links that acceptance to Mrs. Turpin's final glorious vision. The process begins in the doctor's office, when Mrs. Turpin's pride in her moral superiority to Negroes and "white trash" is shattered by the ugly Mary Grace, who first assaults her with a book—*Human Development*—and then calls her a "wart hog from hell." The perverse girl serves as an instrument of divine grace as her name obviously indicates, but her demonic behavior underscores the mystery of the role of evil in the divine plan, particularly the mystery of spiritual transformation effected by a recognition of personal evil. This is a mystery that Mrs. Turpin, in her proud moral self-assurance, has never admitted, but it is brought home to her personally in the question she is forced to ponder after the attack: how can I be a wart hog from hell and be saved too?

On the metaphysical level, this question concerns the mystery of analogy: how can she be like a hog and like God too? Stated differently, how can she be a part of the natural order and a part of the divine as well? Theologically, the question points to the larger mystery of the redemptive process: how can one be corrupt and be saved too? O'Connor's use of the doctrine that, while man is made "in God's image," none of his efforts are self-sufficient for redemption further specifies an analogical view of reality as central to the theological question. Mrs. Turpin can no more save herself by her dutiful good works than can Haze Motes or the Misfit or

Rayber by their actions. In fact, her good deeds may instead prove a stumbling block to salvation if they breed spiritual pride and a constriction of vision in which the mystery of evil in the process of redemption is ignored. Mary Grace's assault on Mrs. Turpin and the probing questions that follow it are meant to awaken this sense of the larger mystery.

Mrs. Turpin is forced to ask herself: how can I be a wart hog and be saved too? The question is analogical on the level of metaphysics, but the specific analogue O'Connor evokes is biblical. Mrs. Turpin's hubristic questioning of God in the latter part of the story ("Who do you think you are?") resembles Job's questioning of God, since she speaks "as if she were defending her innocence to invisible guests who were like the comforters of Job, reasonable-seeming but wrong." Moreover, her situation in life as a dutiful and conscientious citizen resembles Job's, and the questions her new predicament raises are precisely his: why is my good life insufficient for God's favor? what role does evil and suffering play in the final purpose of creation? The response Job receives is of course no answer, only the living mystery of God's power and his love of Job. In his affliction and his debate with the deity, in his resolute refusal of glib explanations, Job comes to embody paradoxically the mystery of man "made in God's image." In creating Mrs. Turpin, O'Connor broadens the vision by combining both the Old Testament analogue of Job with the New Testament analogue of redemption to develop a Christian view of the questions raised by Mrs. Turpin. In this way "Revelation" dramatizes a deeper, more progressive vision of history.

Mrs. Turpin's Job-like questions about her worth and the meaning of her life are answered by her final revelation, a vision of the Christian mystical community:

> A visionary light settled in her eyes. She saw the streak as a vast swinging bridge extending upward from the earth through a field of living fire. Upon it a vast horde of souls were rumbling toward heaven. There were whole companies of white-trash, clean for the first time in their lives, and bands of black niggers in white robes, and battalions of freaks and lunatics shouting and clapping and leaping like frogs. And bringing up the end of the procession was a tribe of people whom she recognized at once as those who, like herself and Claud, had always had a little of everything and the God-given wit to use it right. She leaned forward to observe them closer. They were marching behind the others with great dignity, accountable as they had always been for good order and common sense and respectable behavior. They alone were on key. Yet she

could see by their shocked and altered faces that even their virtues were being burned away. (*Complete Stories*, p. 508)

The answers contained in the hierophany are of course the mysteries addressed by St. Paul: that salvation cannot be equated with good deeds and that "the lame shall enter first." Moreover, this hierophany demonstrates the Christological view of reality, the idea that the dimensions and meaning of the concrete world are ultimately mysterious and that the heart of this mystery is the power of spiritual transformation of the natural order by divine grace. This power of divine love is the unifying force in the mystical community, and Mrs. Turpin sees it at the end of the story with devastating clarity. In creating Mrs. Turpin and her final vision O'Connor herself performed an artistic transformation of earlier motifs depicted in her characterization of farm women, to offer a comprehensive view of mystical community and the end of history.

Chapter Five

History, Memory, and Eschatology

If I had not known you, I would not have found you.
—Pascal, quoted by Flannery O'Connor in "Novelist and Believer"

For some critics of O'Connor's fiction her adherence to a religious view-point that affirms the ultimate fulfillment of the process of redemption in the mystical community necessarily implies her disengagement from history and its struggles. As a corollary to this argument, the case is also made that O'Connor's treatment of the spiritual consciousness of modern man, particularly in his engagement with relativism, is too simplistic and primitive to do full justice to his real condition. Such an argument further implies that O'Connor's peculiar stance separates her from the mainstream of great southern writers in the twentieth century. I shall take up the question of her treatment of consciousness in the next chapter; here, I want to focus on the question of her relationship to the southern literary mainstream and to contemporary history and its implications.

The criticism of O'Connor noted above has been best expressed by Lewis P. Simpson in his brilliant study of the American literary consciousness, *The Brazen Face of History*. Simpson argues that like many of their contemporaries in England and Europe, the major twentieth-century southern writers—Faulkner, Warren, Welty, and others—were confronted with the modern crisis of the "historicism of consciousness," that is, an intellectual crisis which creates a consciousness bent on "looking upon everything—man, nature, place, time, and God—as subject to the dominion of history . . . history as an ineluctable process or series of processes, which may be regarded as teleological or blankly purposeless (pp. 240–41). This crisis had its roots in the breakup of the medieval order in the West and the rise of modernity beginning in the Renaissance, and it involved the "transformation of an assumed metaphysical and moral order into the dehumanized present-day society of history and science."

In reaction to this compulsion toward historicism, which threatens the

very bases of order and identity within the mind, the great southern writers developed an "aesthetic of memory," according to Simpson. Writers
such as Faulkner, Warren, and Welty came to look upon "remembering as
an art of the psychic—the spiritual—survival," and their aesthetic of
memory came into being as a conscious literary mode when the "culture of
kinship and custom, of tradition and myth, began to give way altogether
to the culture of rationality. . . . In this situation, memory became, not a
spiritual heritage, but a 'life's work'" (p. 241). Thus for Simpson the great
southern writers discovered what he sees as the "omnipresent subject of
modern letters: man's idea of himself as a creature of his own conception of
history, and his resistance to this idea" (p. 238).

Simpson argues that such is not the case with Flannery O'Connor. She
rejected the aesthetic of memory because she saw the South's history as a
microcosm of larger universal history, one which the southern writer can
perceive because his vision is essentially prophetic, "a vision of Moses' face
as he pulverized our idols." For O'Connor, the southern writer gifted with
the prophetic vision is, to use Simpson's phrase, "a participant . . . in the
transcendent mystery of the history behind the history," and his problem
as an artist is to discover in his work that "nexus of time, place, and
eternity" which is his true location. But Simpson believes that by rejecting the aesthetic of memory in favor of a "mode of revelation" as a fictional
aesthetic, O'Connor effectively removed herself from the mainstream of
the southern literary imagination and from the modern mind's struggle
with the central issue of the historicism of consciousness:

> Ascribing to the Southern writer a transcendent religiosity of
> consciousness, she parodies the quest to resist the historicist com-
> pulsion. An actor in the drama of existence, lacking the capacity
> for detached observation and suspension of judgment, she fails to
> realize that her concept of a simultaneous descent into the self and
> into the South is a way of evading the historicism of consciousness;
> that the problem of locating the transcendent juncture of time,
> place, and eternity is ironically involved with the problem of the
> modern self's tendency to enclose history in the self. Having no
> empathy with the self that internalizes history as memory so that it
> may survive history and its catastrophes, she oversimplifies the
> modern situation of the self; her stories employ a series of characters
> who lack the sophistication to grapple inwardly with the subtleties
> of the self as a creature of modern history. She lacks, perhaps
> refuses, an intimacy with history. Blessed by an overpowering gift
> of faith, she lets the Faulkner company, the survivors of history, go

its way. Her vision is directed toward timeless order and the ultimate beatitude of the soul. Prophesying the *irresistibility* of God's
grace in the life of the individual, her stories follow a compelling
aesthetic of revelation. The result is that, in spite of their detailed
portrayal of the manners of her region, they divest it of a tension
toward historical reality. (pp. 247–48, my italics)

Although probably no one has put the case against O'Connor's aesthetic
as forcefully as Simpson has in this statement, several preliminary questions can be raised. The first is about his claim that O'Connor's stories
prophesy the *"irresistibility* of God's grace in the life of the individual."
Such a claim seems oversimplified because it fails to distinguish between
the movement whereby many characters are led to a *possible* acceptance of
grace and the actual acceptance itself. There is a crucial difference between
the grace of revelation given to Mr. Head and the Grandmother on the one
hand, for example, and that given to Hulga Hopewell and Asbury Fox on
the other. Simpson's statement seems to ignore the fact that the movement of grace in Hulga and Asbury is a descent into revelation of their
true selves, into their real historical situation, and that what they then
choose to do with that new insight is left open by O'Connor. There is
nothing irresistible about the grace offered, and rather than being a mode
of transcendence for these characters, it is the opposite, a return of themselves which is a downward movement into the immanent, the present
moment, and into history. Moreover, Simpson's remark overlooks characters such as Mr. Fortune and Rayber, who clearly reject the grace offered
and in so doing belie any notion of irresistibility. Therefore, to say that
O'Connor's vision is only directed toward "timeless order" seems to reduce
unduly the complexity of her stories, particularly the dynamic process of
history in tensional relation to the transcendent that she unfolds in the
fiction.

Second, one may well ask whether the central assumption behind Simpson's argument—the idea of the historicism of consciousness—can be regarded as definitive of the modern situation as he suggests. Is such a thesis
too comprehensive a formulation to explain the complex reality of the
twentieth-century historical-literary situation? Does the problem of the
historicism of consciousness necessarily mean that the "culture of kinship
and custom, of tradition and myth, began to give way altogether to the
culture of rationality"? On the contrary, it seems possible to find many
examples of vital belief in a traditionalist religious and metaphysical order
in the modern sensibility, and if these examples do exist they are appropriate subjects for representation in fiction. Indeed, O'Connor has created

this vital belief in characters such as Mrs. Greenleaf, Father Finn, the Carmodys, old Mason Tarwater, and the priest and the Guizacs in "The Displaced Person." One may wish to argue that these characters are exceptions who do not represent the general condition of the modern mind's struggle against the forces of historicism. But such a view only leads to the more fundamental question: whether or not the modern tendency toward historicism precludes *any* access whatsoever to a transcendent order of reality, that divine order revealed in this world as the "history behind the history"? Simpson seems to imply that the answer can only be yes, that "everything—man, nature, place, time and God—[is] subject to the dominion of history." Walker Percy raises the same issue in his essay "Notes for a Novel About the End of the World," when he asks whether the "tempestuous restructuring" of modern consciousness in the twentieth century has made it impossible to hear the Good News.[1] O'Connor's response to this issue and her fictional method in dealing with it show clearly the reasons behind her rejection of the so-called Southern aesthetic of memory as a completely satisfactory and viable response to the modern situation.

It seems that the critical point of difference between O'Connor and the group of southern writers Simpson identifies as employing an aesthetic of memory concerns the question of the nature and function of memory itself. Simpson's use of the term implies a definition of memory as a wholly natural human faculty, one which is effective as a defensive stratagem or weapon against the loss of a culture of kinship and custom, tradition, and myth. This view sees the faculty of memory—a powerful faculty: engaged in "psychic and spiritual survival"—exclusively in terms of its function within the natural order. Yet if this is the range of memory, one might well ask how memory is to be powerful enough to resist the compulsion toward historicism. Since in this definition memory is itself solely a mode of natural human consciousness, how can it be capable of transcending the historicism of consciousness? I would call such a characterization "historicist memory" in spite of its claim, paradoxically, to be a means to resist the forces of historicism. Certainly Simpson is correct in noting how it became a dominant aesthetic strategy in general in the twentieth century, particularly among major southern writers. However, such a characterization does not seem inclusive enough to denote the full capacities of memory, for in O'Connor's case particularly the concept of memory extends beyond the natural order and must be understood as a faculty that engages the mysterious dynamics of relationship between the immanent and the transcendent, between history and eschatology.

In discussing the way in which the human intellect is illuminated by

God, Etienne Gilson, echoing St. Augustine, speaks of "metaphysical memory," the mode by which the Divine "attests His intimate presence in me."[2] According to this view, memory is a natural faculty but one whose roots reach ultimately into the transcendent, into our knowledge of "unchangeable Truth," particularly the truth of our condition as contingent beings who exist by virtue of our participation in the divine. Hence Pascal's observation: "If I had not known you, I would not have found you." In short, in this view metaphysical memory is intimately involved in the mystery of our intuitive knowledge of God. Gilson argues, in fact, that it is impossible for us to make true judgments unless we know not only what "a thing is" but also what it "ought to be," that is, know it according to its rule or norm, which is "the divine idea" in which it participates and strives to imitate. This basis of judgment is rooted in the reality of metaphysical memory.

This larger notion of memory must be used when discussing O'Connor's fiction because most often her protagonists are involved in an action of spiritual *recollection*; in a literal way, these characters are being recalled by some events to the true source and nature of themselves as created beings. In the case of the Grandmother or Mrs. Shortley, for example, it is an action of metaphysical memory that William Lynch describes as an action of "comic remembrance." He emphasizes that such a movement is essentially analogical because through it men "recall the relationship between God and themselves."[3] He also describes, as I have noted earlier, how this anamnesis is often accomplished by "foreshortening," an apt description of O'Connor's use of shock and violence to achieve the effect of "comic remembrance."

In contrast to this idea of metaphysical memory, the aesthetic of historicist memory employed by many southern writers as a means of order against the forces of historicism seems inadequate because this form of memory is a mode of consciousness which, by itself, is incapable of transcending the historicist compulsion. As part of a process of human intellectuality, viewed *exclusively* in natural terms, it is subject to the mind's own fallibility as well as memory's tendency toward selectivity and exaggeration. That O'Connor well understood this limitation of historicist memory is clear, I think, from "A Late Encounter with the Enemy." George Poker Sash has been "recreated" as General Tennessee Flintrock Sash through his own and others' impulse to romanticize history. This impulse constitutes a denial of true history and of Sash's real situation in both past and present. Against this distortion O'Connor affirms a truer historical sense in the words of the commencement speaker in the story: "If we forget our past . . . we won't remember our future and it will be as well for we won't have one" (*Complete Stories*, p. 142). But even this more accurate memory of history, valuable as it is, is insufficient for man. General Sash struggles to deny his true past, which has been reawakened by the speaker's words, and he dies trying to escape death, the "black procession" that has haunted all his days. His attempt to escape is analogous to Julian's attempted escape from the truth of history at the end of "Everything That Rises Must Converge." Their efforts are attempts to escape the fullness of memory, that is, the metaphysical knowledge of their truly contingent existence. O'Connor recalls them to this fullness of memory by way of comic action. The acts of comic remembrance which they undergo when Sash unwillingly faces death and Julian is faced with the death of his mother are actions which do not derive from their own consciousness and in fact undermine their presumed states of consciousness. The distinction is crucial because it speaks to a central assumption in Simpson's argument and helps clarify O'Connor's difference from other modern southern writers.

Simpson's understanding of southern writers' conscious use of an aesthetic of memory also assumes, as I noted, that the historicism of consciousness is *the* modern problem and that consciousness therefore tends to become identified with the whole of reality. O'Connor categorically rejected such a view. In her essays, letters, and fiction, she constantly condemned those for whom reality began and ended with the borders of their skulls. Again and again the false god of presumed self-sufficient reason is attacked: in Rayber and Sheppard and Hulga, in Asbury Fox and Julian and Haze Motes and Mr. Head. These characters' attempts to limit reality to the dimensions of their own minds are confounded at every turn by comic action, comic remembrance dramatized analogically. In every case, O'Connor shatters the idol of solipsistic consciousness and forces these protagonists to encounter that larger reality governed by mystery. For her, the life of consciousness and of historicist memory alone as a mode of order and transcendence was too limited both as a subject for fiction and as an artistic stance, too narrow to encompass the full reality of man's true situation in history. Her view is closer to that expressed by Mircea Eliade in *Images and Symbols: Studies in Religious Symbolism:*

> The terms "history" and "historic" can occasion much confusion; they indicate, on the one hand, all that is *concrete* and *authentic* in a given human existence, as opposed to the inauthentic existence constituted by evasions and automatisms of every kind. On the other hand, in various historicist and existentialist currents of thought, "history" and "historic" seem to imply that human exis-

tence is authentic only insofar as it is reduced to the *awakened consciousness of its historic moment*. It is to the latter, the "totalitarian" meaning of history that I am referring when I take issue against "historicisms." It seems to me, indeed, *that the authenticity of an existence cannot be limited to the consciousness of its own historicity;* one cannot regard as "evasive" or "inauthentic," the fundamental experiences of love, anxiety, joy, melancholy, etc. Each of these make use of a temporal rhythm proper to itself, and all combine to constitute what might be called the integral man, who neither denies himself to his historic moment, nor consents to be identified with it. (pp. 171–72, my italics)

But the deeper question raised by Simpson's notion of the internalization of history in consciousness remains. The question concerns O'Connor's attempt to evoke the history behind the history—the transcendent order of reality which encompasses and gives meaning to history. From her writings it is evident that she was well aware of the problem of the historicism of consciousness, the process of making history immanent within the self, the rationalistic imperative that so saturates contemporary existence as to make awareness of the transcendent, immutable reality extremely difficult:

For the last two centuries we have lived in a world which has been increasingly convinced that the reaches of reality end very close to the surface, that there is no ultimate divine source. . . . For nearly two centuries the popular spirit of each succeeding generation has tended more and more to the view that the mysteries of life will eventually fall before the mind of man. Many modern novelists have been more concerned with the processes of consciousness than with the objective world outside the mind. In twentieth-century fiction it increasingly happens that a meaningless, absurd world impinges upon the sacred consciousness of author or character; author and character seldom now go out to explore and penetrate a world in which the sacred is reflected. (*Mystery and Manners,* pp. 157–58)

Awareness of the transcendent reality may indeed have become difficult, as Percy suggests, but not impossible; O'Connor rejected any idea of a complete "closure" of man from the divine. Her problem as a writer, however, was to find ways to break through this condition of closure which had been created by the very force of the historicism of consciousness, the modern tendency to identify self, mind, and all reality.

That she believed a transcendent metaphysical and spiritual order could not be recovered by historicist memory alone is I think apparent from her fiction. In addition to "A Late Encounter with the Enemy," frequently in her stories we meet putative Christians—such as Mrs. Hitchock in *Wise Blood,* Mrs. May in "Greenleaf," the Grandmother in "A Good Man is Hard to Find," and Mrs. Cope in "A Circle in the Fire"—who attempt to appropriate Christianity through historicist memory, identifying it with the self and with history. Christianity for them has become only another datum of history. O'Connor's devastating description of Mrs. May typifies this kind of mind: "She was a good Christian woman with a large respect for religion, though she did not, of course, believe any of it was true" (*Complete Stories,* p. 316). But such spiritual decadence will not do for O'Connor; she attacks this rationalizing process by pulverizing the idol her characters have made of Christianity in attempting to reduce its mystery to a mode of human consciousness. To pulverize this idol of consciousness and reveal the history behind the history, O'Connor adopted violence, as a "foreshortening" means of "comic remembrance," as a way of both revealing and speaking to what Eliade calls the "integral man" who is in history but not completely identified with it:

> I suppose the reasons for the use of so much violence in modern fiction will differ with each writer who uses it, but in my own stories I have found that violence is strangely capable of *returning my characters to reality* and preparing them to accept their moment of grace. Their heads are so hard that almost nothing else will do the work. This idea, that reality is *something to which we must be returned at considerable cost,* is one which is seldom understood by the casual reader, but it is one which is implicit in the Christian view of the world." (p. 112, my italics)

As her remark suggests, O'Connor's fictional stance was not based exclusively on the dynamic of memory and history as in other southern writers but rather on the dynamic of history and eschatology.

Because for O'Connor the roots of man's being are anagogical, mind is not the whole self. Yet we find many of her characters already imbued with the historicist disease. One need only look at the state of mind represented in Rayber, Hulga Hopewell, Asbury Fox, Mrs. McIntyre, and the Misfit to see this condition clearly. Perhaps best dramatized in Haze Motes's gospel of the Church Without Christ when he proclaims, "Nothing outside you can give you any place. . . . In yourself right now is all the place you've got" (*Three by Flannery O'Connor,* p. 90), this condition constitutes such a reductive, closed view of reality that O'Connor felt impelled to use violence as a means of reestablishing the larger, more complex vision of reality. I would argue that rather than evading history and the problem of historicism, she recast history within a larger framework, at the same time revealing the very limitations of mind by itself to transcend the historicist compulsion.

To envision the kind of mind created by O'Connor's use of violence and "comic remembrance," we must imagine the state of Hulga Hopewell's, Asbury Fox's, and Julian's minds *after* their shocks of recognition. As I have already suggested, these characters will continue to live in the world—in history—with their new self-knowledge, and it is difficult to imagine them as intellectually unsophisticated. Moreover, these characters gain an immense power to act because the vital dimension which is established by the violence in her stories is the power of freedom, that terrifying freedom which is at the core of the tension between history and eschatology—the freedom to accept or reject divine grace which has absolute consequences.

The New Testament notion of the tension between history and eschatology is important to recall here for two reasons: first, because it is so central to the Christian conception of history and antithetical to the idea of the historicism of consciousness as a completely adequate interpretation of history; and second, because it so accurately describes the tension between history and eschatology created in O'Connor's work, a tension founded on the scriptural thesis.

The full meaning of the scriptural concept of eschatology continues to be debated but several of its essential features can be elucidated here. As the theologian John L. McKenzie has pointed out, the basic definition of eschatology involves "the belief that history issues in a divine act which terminates history and inaugurates a new age, a new dimension of reality."[4] The concept of eschatology is a biblical answer to the problem of dualism, particularly the dualism inherent in the conflict between history as process and the idea of transcendent, absolute spiritual order. The aesthetic of memory noted by Simpson is another response to that dualism, but one that I think is finally incapable of resolving that dualism because its source, especially since Descartes, is too exclusively within the mind, too conditioned by historical process.

The complicating factor in the notion of eschatology is, of course, the Incarnation, Christ's entry into history. With this event human destiny achieves its fully eschatological and historical character. On the one hand, Christ is an eschatological figure whose coming inaugurates a new age— the Reign of God. McKenzie notes in *The Power and the Wisdom:* "The New Testament speaks with conviction of the fullness of revelation in Jesus Christ; and the church has always understood that there cannot be another gospel. He begins the last age." On the other hand, this tendency toward the fulfillment of human destiny cannot be conceived as separate from the function and goal of human destiny in the world—in history. In spite of the paradox, "both characters must be retained," and "when this is understood, one feels that the tension between history and eschatology has become more acute" (p. 81). This tension derives from a biblical conception of history, which "sees the present as both recapitulating the entire past and as implicitly containing the entire future" (p. 84). Eliade states the same paradox as follows:

> And yet it must not be lost sight of, that Christianity entered History in order to abolish it: the greatest hope of the Christian is the second coming of Christ, which is to put an end to all History. From a certain point of view, for every Christian individually, this end, and the eternity to follow it—the paradise regained—may be attained *from this moment. The time to come* announced by Christ is already accessible, and for him who has regained it, history ceases to be. The transformation of Time into Eternity began with the first believers. (*Images and Symbols,* p. 172)

O'Connor dramatizes this tension in the ending of *The Violent Bear It Away,* for though young Tarwater receives the transcendent vision of his great-uncle resurrected in glory, he still must follow out his earthly vocation, to enter the "dark city" and "warn the children of God of the terrible speed of God's mercy."

What is particularly crucial in the eschatological thesis, and indeed in the whole Christian conception of the redemption of history, is that fulfillment is not seen in individualistic terms. Rather, as I have argued in chapter 4, fulfillment is viewed in terms of an ideal of corporate union, the mystical community. The Christian concept of history and eschatology is the traditional orthodoxy O'Connor believed in, yet she saw everywhere resistance to this corporate destiny, particularly in the form of those who retreat into the world of solitary mind. Consequently, she used shock and violence to attack this situation of closure, with its tendency to internalize history within the self; she enacts comic remembrance and awakens in her characters that deeper metaphysical memory of their place in the larger order of reality. Not all of her characters accept this radical awakening. But she gave them and her readers the freedom to see it, to experience the complex dynamic between eschatology and history, and to live as creators of history and not merely its victims. That it took violence to make possible this larger vision may seem unfortunate, but, like Walker Percy, O'Connor well understood that it was too late in the day for a simple aesthetic of memory to serve as a viable fictional stance.

Chapter Six

Risen Sons: History, Consciousness, and Personality

Anyone familiar with the critical canon that has developed around the work of Flannery O'Connor is aware that there are profound differences in the judgments about her fiction. Some of these differences concern questions of execution—of measuring the distance, as it were, between the stories themselves and the explicit theological vision of her essays and letters. Other differences stem from questioning O'Connor's vision itself: in particular, whether the vision is sufficiently complex to deal with the subtle nuances of the modern mind's spiritual struggles, or conversely, whether her vision represents an archaism, a reactionary oversimplification of the spiritual problems of modernity. We know that she was generally hostile to the "prevailing spirit" of the times. Was that hostility so strong in her as to induce a refusal to confront the full implications of the modern mind's predicament? Such is the argument, as I have already noted, Lewis Simpson makes in *The Brazen Face of History* when he charges that O'Connor "oversimplifies the modern situation of the self; her stories employ a series of characters who lack the sophistication to grapple inwardly with the subtleties of the self as a creature of modern secular history. She lacks, perhaps refuses, an intimacy with history" (pp. 244–48).

The central issue raised by Simpson's criticism concerns in the broadest sense the question of the representation of reality in O'Connor's stories: whether or not this representation is true to the dimensions and possibilities of existence as we know it. Although from a literary standpoint the issue must be engaged within the stories themselves by examination of language and structure, the issue cannot be understood exclusively in literary terms. The stories themselves presuppose a certain history and a certain metaphysical view of reality and human nature which are prior to and in the sense "outside of" the stories. From a literary standpoint the meaning of those views may only be validated within the stories themselves, but the meaning is inseparable from the larger intellectual context from which those views derive.

To approach this question of the representation of reality in O'Connor's stories necessarily calls for some discussion of her Christian faith as a starting point. Throughout this study I have argued that O'Connor's sense of reality, her vision of history, and her fictional technique are inseparable because they derive from a single source: her belief in Christ's Incarnation, death, and Resurrection. For a believer such as O'Connor the Christ event is *the* event in history. It not only radically changed the direction and meaning of history but also transformed the whole order and possibilities inherent in being. Consequently, the Christ event has a revolutionary effect on the meaning of human personality, including of course the nature and dimensions of consciousness. These aspects of O'Connor's thought, as shaped by her belief in the Christ event, I now want to focus upon in order to explore more fully the question of the representation of reality in her fiction.

This problem is compounded by O'Connor's apparent confirmation of the view that her characters represent deliberate simplifications on her part. In a letter to her friend "A," she commented on her ability to create a Hulga Hopewell but not a character as intellectually sophisticated as Simone Weil: "You have to be able to dominate the existence that you characterize. That is why I write about people who are more or less primitive. I can't dominate a Miss Weil because she is more intelligent and better than I am but I can project a Hulga" (*The Habit of Being*, p. 106). If true, such a statement would seem to confirm Simpson's criticism of O'Connor's work. But of course her remark deprecates her immensely complex and sophisticated mind, one steeped, as Marion Montgomery has shown in *Why Flannery O'Connor Stayed Home*, in the major intellectual currents of the past and the twentieth century. This complex "mind," it seems to me, is fully revealed in her fiction. To put the matter differently, O'Connor's remark about the "primitiveness" of her characters, taken in isolation, ignores the *total* reality that constituted their fictional milieu, the whole order of being represented in the story, which involves the external world of place, the dimension of time, conflict, and evolving dramatic relationships, as well as character.[1] Her characters should not be measured in isolation because the relationships between self and world, mind and external reality, person and history are of the essence of her dramatic vision. O'Connor may dominate her characters in a sense as a creative artist, but because her field of vision impinges upon mystery, in a deeper sense she cannot, indeed dare not, dominate them. To achieve the ends of her fiction, the creation of mystery, required openness and freedom.

Given her theological viewpoint, it seems inadequate to defend the "primitiveness" of her characters with the traditional critical argument that hers was a comic art given to distortion, caricaturization, and over-simplification of character. From the standpoint of literary genre, O'Connor was certainly adept at what William Lynch describes as "comic fore-shortening." Nevertheless, this technique alone does not speak to the central issue of the meaning of human personality and consciousness in her work. This technique is especially inadequate because of O'Connor's commitment to represent either openly or by implication the struggle in humanity precipitated by Christ's entry into history. Anything she wished to dramatize about this struggle necessarily involved the whole question of the development, complexities, and possibilities inherent in personality. As such, her creation of characters resists simple categorization according to a tradition of literary types, comic or otherwise.

What can be said, then, about the nature of personality and consciousness represented in characters such as Hulga Hopewell, Mrs. Shortley, Enoch Emery, the Misfit, young Tarwater, Asbury Fox, and others? And how can the various "levels" of consciousness or degrees of complexity be understood in relation to the concepts of personality and history that derive from a belief in Christ's Incarnation and Resurrection? The integral nature of the question seems apparent: one cannot discuss Christ's impact on human consciousness without considering how his presence trans-formed the meaning and possibilities of human personality, and this in turn cannot be separated from the effects of his presence on the meaning and direction of history. The issue is of course extraordinarily complex, and full discussion is impossible within the scope of this study. Nevertheless, in order to establish a more accurate sense of the meaning of character in O'Connor's work, I want to undertake a preliminary discussion, albeit in summary fashion, of some of the theological and philosophical roots of her Christology.

Notions about the nature of human personality and the development of consciousness are necessarily bound up with philosophies of history. With regard to O'Connor, it is important to sketch out some of the intellectual paths followed by several twentieth-century thinkers, particularly Eric Voegelin, Mircea Eliade, Etienne Gilson, Jacques Maritain, Karl Jaspers, William Lynch, Claude Tresmontant, and William Thompson.[2] O'Connor was familiar with most of these philosophers either directly or indirectly from her reading; she acknowledged a great debt to some, Gilson and Maritain, for example, in the development of her own thought. These and others helped her arrive at a philosophy of history which became the governing inspiration in her development of fictional characters.

The radical impact of the Christ event can best be seen in terms of attempts to understand the order and meaning of history. On this question Jaspers, Eliade, Voegelin, and others speak in various ways of an original cosmological or mythical order of being characterized by a *oneness* in the sense of being; man feels himself to be in union with the cosmos, the world of nature and the gods. *Self*-consciousness and the sense of individual differentiation it begets do not exist. Thompson asserts that man's consciousness in this mythical order is governed by projection, fantasy, and wish-fulfillment. He further distinguishes a second and subsequent order of existence which he terms "conventional," an order that emerged culturally with the increasing complication of society and which is characterized by a marked increase in the degree of rationality and the use of abstraction by man. Slowly man begins to differentiate himself from nature. Jaspers calls this a process of "spiritualization" in the psychic development of man. However, man still defines himself and understands his worth in terms of society and its governing values and patterns of behavior, hence the term "conventional." As yet man has not "broken through" to the notions of full individuation, self-autonomy, and freedom.[3]

The crucial breakthrough in the development of human consciousness, which Jaspers calls the "axial" breakthrough and Voegelin refers to as a "leap in being," occurred somewhere between 800 and 300 B.C.[4] Voegelin sees four specific "leaps": in Israel, through Moses and the prophets; in Greece, among the philosophers from Parmenides to Aristotle; in India, through the Buddha and Mahavira; and in China, through Confucius and Lao-tzu. For the purpose of focusing on the Christ event, our attention here must necessarily center on Israel. In general, this axial breakthrough or "leap in being" is one in which man achieves a new spiritual perception of a higher, more authentically personal mode of existence. Voegelin calls this breakthrough an act of "differentiation" on man's part, a greater insight into the nature and order of reality than previously achieved. Of crucial significance is the source and nature of this insight. According to Voegelin, its source is a divine revelation, as a result of which man can now understand himself as a participant in a transcendent and divine reality beyond the order of nature and society. He is thus called to a personal relationship with the divine being, who initiates the call out of love for His creation.

From the standpoint of the development of human consciousness and personality, this "leap in being" is characterized by a new *self*-awareness on man's part—a greater sense of the power of rationality through which differentiation occurs, a heightened sense of individual freedom, and an intensified sense of self-responsibility. For Voegelin, Thompson, and others, this breakthrough into higher human consciousness necessarily involves a perception of the divine being as the very *source* of individuation. When this perception is reached a "conversion" occurs in which man senses himself in partnership with God. He can actively co-create history and be responsible for it; he is not merely a subject who passively receives history's imprint. As we shall see later, these ideas are linchpins in the Christian concept of personality and history.

A complicating factor in this view of the development of human consciousness in history concerns the whole question of chronology and the metaphysic of time itself in relation to the transcendent. While it is impossible to treat the question fully here, some fundamental notions must be mentioned as bearing directly on any discussion of the Christ event, particularly in relation to characters in O'Connor's fiction. First, although Jaspers, Voegelin, and others appear to conceive of the axial breakthrough to higher, more individuated consciousness chronologically, as a "stage" in historical development, this development should not be seen simply as evolutionary. The term "evolution" suggests an irreversible process and by implication a rather deterministic view of history. Voegelin himself has moved away from his earlier notion of stages of history and of clear distinctions between periods in favor of a more vertical view.[5] That is, for him the breakthrough to higher human consciousness made possible by divine revelation, although dated during the period 800–300 B.C., is transhistorical by virtue of the fact that it involves an irruption of the divine in history and the human psyche. This revelation transfigures the meaning of time and history in relation to the eternal transcendent; it is a revelation of the mystery of being. Consequently, a higher, more differentiated human consciousness should be viewed as a possibility for man. And even if a higher consciousness is achieved, there is nothing to preclude a relapse into lower modes of existence, what Voegelin calls a reversion into archaism.

Secondly, the idea of the vertical view of the development of consciousness, of deepening possibilities of human personality, does not mean a complete superceding of the mythical and conventional modes. Rather, as Thompson points out, the vertical view of the breakthrough allows for a higher, more rational integration of these levels by a process of complication of consciousness. It should be noted, of course, that this vertical view of human psychic development and history is at the heart of the typological strategy of O'Connor's art and that its metaphysical basis is the doctrine of the analogy of being. In many stories O'Connor quite consciously creates these various levels of meaning simultaneously—mythical, conventional, and Christian—within specific images and actions, while always pushing the story toward a wider frame of meaning and mystery without negating another level. That is, she pushes the story ultimately toward an expression of what Voegelin calls "the mystery in the structure of history," which O'Connor identified as the goal of her fiction:

> If the writer believes that our life is and will remain essentially mysterious, if he looks upon us as beings existing in a created order to whose laws we freely respond, then what he sees on the surface will be of interest to him only as he can go through it into an experience of mystery itself. His kind of fiction will always be pushing its own limits outward toward the limits of mystery, because for this kind of writer, the meaning of a story does not begin except at a depth where adequate motivation and adequate psychology and various determinations have been exhausted. Such a writer will be interested in what we don't understand rather than in what we do. He will be interested in possibility rather than probability. (*Mystery and Manners,* p. 41)

Voegelin describes the new dimension of possibility in the order of being and human consciousness which is created by the axial breakthrough as an experience of *metaxy.* That is, man now senses himself as being "in-Between" the One and the Many. The experience of metaxy—the tensional, mysterious relationship between God and man—is for Voegelin "the drama of mankind." In the metaxy there is no "length of time" in which things happen. Instead there is "the reality of things which has a time dimension." Rather than being a series of events occurring in chronological fashion, history as a whole is seen as a new "horizon of divine mystery" in which man responds freely to the theophanic revelations.

At the center of this view of history is the meaning of consciousness itself, its discovery, as Gerhart Niemeyer has noted, of "its own movements as events in history." Commenting on Voegelin's discussion of the axial breakthrough, Niemeyer stresses the importance of "the openness of consciousness toward that 'eminent' reality which is 'more real' than things." Such a consciousness is firmly grounded in reason: "In this openness the world with its 'things' becomes intelligible. 'The life of reason,' concludes Voegelin, 'is thus firmly rooted in a revelation.'"[6] As I shall argue later, this openness of consciousness to the mysterious, to the reality more real than things, is both cause and aim in O'Connor's fiction. As an artist she attempts to create the world of mystery in her stories; at the same time, the drama of her protagonists' minds is their acceptance or refusal of openness to that mystery. Like Voegelin, she specifically links the belief in mystery to the highest possibilities of human reason, arguing that her stories involved a "reasonable use of the unreasonable."

Although Voegelin sees the discovery of metaxy as characteristic of the axial breakthrough in general and not exclusively rooted in the Christ event, he finds in the writings of St. Paul the fullest, most "differentiated" perception of the meaning of the divine revelation and of the direction and goal of history. Insofar as Christian theology is concerned, the "mystery in the structure of history" revealed in the axial breakthrough is rooted in Christ's Incarnation, death, and Resurrection. The Christ event revealed the full meaning of time in relation to eternity; Christ's coming inaugurated a new age and revealed the eschatalogical structure of history. Moreover, it made possible a new dimension of human freedom in the drama of mankind.

Commenting on the axial breakthrough in relation to the Gospels and St. Paul's writings, Thompson indicates at least three specific effects of the Christ event on this new level of consciousness, all of which make possible a higher degree of differentiation or individuation for men.[7] First, Christ's coming into history intensified man's awareness of a *personal* God, who reveals himself to man through love. Second, his crucifixion and death reveal the ultimate meaning of human freedom and self-responsibility in history. Third, and most important because it radically separates the Christ event from other revelations, Christ's Resurrection *completed* the axial breakthrough. It created in the believer a heightened sense of the transcendent source of personal identity, beyond mutability and all the oppressive powers of the world. All the destructive powers arrayed against individual personality are subsumed under and made relative by the Resurrection. And concomitant with the resurrection belief was a new power to act creatively in the world, to direct history in freedom and self-responsibility.

For the Christian believer such as O'Connor, the possibility for the fullest realization of human personality is inseparable, then, from the meaning of Christ's Incarnation and Resurrection. He is the image of the whole man, the Son of man, who explored the full dimensions of human existence. Such a belief is cogently summarized by Maritain:

> It is in a theological form, and at the peak of the most abstract conceptualization, that the notions of person and personality were first explicitly offered to the human mind: namely, in the dogmatic formulas concerned with Christian faith in the divine Trinity—one Nature in Three Persons—and in the Incarnation of the Word—a

divine Person assuming human nature. At the same time the
human mind was confronted with a new idea of man—the Gospels
of St. Paul disclosed to it the prevalence of the internal man over
the external man, of the inner life of the soul over legal or exterior
forms—and it could contemplate in the Son of Man crowned with
thorns the abysmal depths of the most living and mysterious Self.
(_Creative Intuition in Art and Poetry_, p. 20)

Looking at the possibilities of human personality from the point of view of
biblical metaphysics, Etienne Gilson similarly underscores the Christocentric roots of the dimensions of being:

How could personality be anything but the mark of being at the
very summit of its perfection, in a philosophy like the Christian
philosophy where everything is suspended from the creative act of a
personal God? For all things were made by the Word, and the
Word is with God, and the Word is God; that is to say precisely
this being who represents Himself as personal in virtue of the sole
fact that He represents Himself as Being: . . . _ego sum qui sum._
Christian personalism also, like the rest, has its roots in the metaphysics of Exodus; we are persons because we are the work of a
Person; we participate in His personality even as, being good, we
participate in His perfection; being causes, in His creative power;
being prudent, in His providence; and, in a word, as beings in His
being. (_The Spirit of Medieval Philosophy_, pp. 204–5)

For the Christian believer, then, the Christ event is the pivotal event in
the breakthrough to higher, more individuated consciousness for man. It
defines the full meaning and possibilities of history and personality. However, many philosophers of history concede that a second axial breakthrough, a further complication of human consciousness, occurred roughly
between the period 1200 to 1700 A.D. In this second breakthrough, man
became more intensely self-conscious of himself, more self-reflective. His
own consciousness itself became the immediate and pervasive subject of his
reflection. As a result, he became dramatically aware of his own subjec-
tivity, of himself as the free and active cause of his own thought and
existence, and of his seemingly unmitigated power over nature. In short, he
achieved historical consciousness. He perceived that human existence was
historically conditioned, that man truly _makes_ his own history. With this
historical self-consciousness came the ascendency of secular reason as an
autonomous force in human affairs. From the standpoint of personality,

historical consciousness brought man the sense that he is largely a self-creative being, able to change himself as well as external nature. This consciousness intensified the sense of human possibility *in this world,* of autonomous freedom, and of self-responsibility for history in incalculable ways. By general consensus this breakthrough witnesses the beginning of modern consciousness.

Like Christian consciousness, this historical consciousness did not necessarily become universal but rather came into existence as a possibility for man, a new way of envisioning and understanding experience. The evidence of history suggests that historical consciousness has become the dominant mode of thought in the West since the Enlightenment. However, even though this new historical consciousness implied a different view of history and personality, it cannot be construed as completely incompatible with the Christian vision of man and history. As Thompson has noted, one of the dangers open to the post-Resurrection Christian mind was a tendency toward dualism, a denigration of this world in favor of the transcendent. In this situation, Christian openness to history would be abandoned, and the Christian vision itself would be reduced to the level of a conventional, prescriptive mode of existence. One of the benefits made possible to the Christian vision by historical consciousness was the undermining of such dualism and a reinforcing, as it were, of the necessity for a truly incarnational view of experience and human history. At the same time, on the level of personality, historical consciousness made possible for the individual a more complex, subjective sense of his personal relationship with the divine. Again, we must stress it as a possibility; the particular direction that this new consciousness took historically was in large part quite different.

As we are well aware from our contemporary perspective, the breakthrough to historical consciousness is at the root of the profound spiritual crisis in the West since the late Middle Ages and the decline of Christendom. With the achievement of historical consciousness man seems to become the supreme agent in history, creating and governing events solely through the power of secular reason. History appears to be a totally immanent reality. Everything—God, nature, events—seems capable of being subsumed in the mind, as Simpson has shown.[8] For the mind so disposed, notions of a transcendent order of reality seem obsolete and create what Voegelin has called the condition of "closure," the sense of existence as being totally confined within the mundane order. If belief in a transcendent order persists after the breakthrough to historical consciousness, such belief is often regarded as an archaism, a wish-fulfillment or relapse committed by a mind unwilling to face the full implications of historical consciousness. After all, the new mind argues, is not Christianity itself completely historically conditioned? And as such does it not represent, as Freud and Marx claimed, a shackling convention that must be gone beyond in order to achieve full human individuation and autonomy?

To raise such questions is to point to the central issue surrounding this breakthrough to historical consciousness: whether or not it is an authentic breakthrough, a true "leap in being" which creates a greater differentiation in human personality and consciousness, a further refinement in the possibilities of being? On the whole Voegelin does not think so. He regards it instead as leading to a deformation in being, a state of gnosis in which reason is cut loose from its concrete source in divine revelation. The flaw in historical consciousness then becomes the identification of mind with the whole self and with being (Descartes's "Cogito, ergo sum") and the identification of consciousness with all reality. Gilson echoes Voegelin's ideas of a deformation of being and of closure by noting the loss of the possibility of transcendence implicit in this new mind:

> We have here, indeed, one of the most extraordinary spectacles in the history of thought; the first act opened with Descartes and the play still proceeds. The Christian philosophers were certainly persuaded that nature was made for man, and in this sense it is true to say that man stands at the center of the medieval world; but they recognized, none the less, that since the universe was created by God it is endowed with an existence proper to itself, it is something that man could know but could never pretend to have created. . . . It was only in a local sense that medieval man thought himself to be at the center of things; the whole creation of which he was the destined crown and end, which he recapitulated in himself, was none the less something outside himself, something to which he had to submit and conform himself if he would know anything of its nature. But modern man, brought up on Kantian idealism, regards nature as being no more than an outcome of the laws of the mind. Losing all their independence as divine works, things gravitate henceforth round human thought, whence their laws are derived. What wonder, after that, if criticism has resulted in the virtual disappearance of all metaphysics? If we would pass beyond the physical order there must first be a physical order. If we would rise above nature there must first of all be a nature. As soon as the universe is reduced to the laws of the mind, man, now become creator, has no longer any means of rising above himself. Legislator of a world to which his own mind has given birth, he is henceforth

the prisoner of his own work, and he will never escape from it anymore. (*The Spirit of Medieval Philosophy,* pp. 245–46)

To raise the question of the relationship between the new mind created by historical consciousness and Christian consciousness is to point to one of the central philosophical and theological problems of the past 400 years. I do not intend to discuss that issue here; however I want to add a note relevant to O'Connor. Thompson argues that the mind infused with historical consciousness has followed one path, secular humanism, which has clearly proved a dead end. Because in this form of differentiation the mind itself became the sole criterion of reality, humanism has only led to modern alienation. Incapable of self-transcendence under humanism, his consciousness closed to the full possibilities of being, man's supposed freedom is but a faint shadow of that true metaphysical freedom grounded in the transcendent eternal. Such is the predicament noted by Walker Percy in *Love in the Ruins* when he asks: "Why does humanism lead to bestialism?" Having become their own gods, such secular humanists in fact suffer from what the psychoanalyst Erich Neumann calls "sclerosis of consciousness," in which "the concept of God . . . derives wholly from the sphere of consciousness—or purports to derive from it, as the ego is deluded enough to pretend. [In this condition] there is no longer anything transpersonal, but only personal; there are no more archtypes, but only concepts; no more symbols, only signs."9

This moral, philosophical, and theological situation created by the confrontation between historical and Christian consciousness is, I would argue, the central religious issue that runs through all of O'Connor's major stories. The task she set herself as a writer was to represent faithfully the fact of historical consciousness, which she saw as dominating the modern temper, and yet represent it in such a way *both* to show clearly how it is a deformation of being and at the same time to reveal the possibility of breakthrough to a higher, more complex level of consciousness. Such a revelation would at least open her characters—if only in defeat—to the possibility of self-transcendence and a more authentic personality rooted in the divine. In the stories, as I have tried to suggest, violence becomes the means of disrupting the condition of closure in order to create these possibilities, for a world of possibility is a world governed by the mystery of being that she so forcefully reveals to the reader.

This lengthy but necessarily schematic background concerning theories of the development of consciousness in history seems to me essential to any discussion of mind in O'Connor's characters. The background is especially pertinent for the question of whether or not her characters represent simplifications of the modern consciousness or a refusal on her part to engage contemporary history. Before I turn to the stories themselves, however, two observations are in order. First, although certain characters must be isolated for purposes of discussion, O'Connor's development of character cannot in fact be separated from the whole order of reality in which her characters exist. True for any writer, this fact of inseparability is especially true in O'Connor's case, because the drama in her stories so often *is* precisely the struggle of human consciousness vis-à-vis the mysterious order of reality outside the mind. As I stated at the beginning of this study, her stories constantly raise one question: what does it mean to be a person in history? Second, although discussion of O'Connor's characters here necessarily means talking about them in relation to types or levels of consciousness and the stages they go through, her characters are not merely conceptual models or ideograms for theories of mind and history. As characters they are instances of the living mystery of human personality grounded in the divine. Discussion can shed light upon that mystery, but it cannot reduce to the level of concept the mysterious dynamisms in those characters. As readers we experience that secret sense within them and that "radiance of form" which Maritain says makes them intelligible precisely *as* mysteries.[10]

When we look at O'Connor's stories themselves, at both individual characters and at the whole order of reality that constitutes the total effect of the story, what kind of consciousness does the reader witness? The question is, I think, much more complicated than O'Connor's remark about the primitiveness of her characters would suggest. What is strikingly apparent is that O'Connor envelops the minds of individual characters and infuses the stories with an enormously complex narrative consciousness which governs the whole order of reality in the story. Every element in the story—character, symbol, dramatic action, language—derives from this consciousness. This consciousness is a *presence* in the story, a constant source of intelligibility and order, characterized by openness to the possibilities of being, by freedom, by creative action, and by respect for mystery, particularly the mystery of theophany. The world or order of reality that the consciousness creates is an image of history. The story itself *is* history, and this governing consciousness fulfills the prophetic role of both enacting and revealing in time (the narrative movement itself) the creative action of freedom made possible by that vision of history. In short, this governing consciousness is a modern Christian consciousness, infused with all the nuances and possibilities of a post-axial, post-Resurrection mind that has absorbed the effects of the breakthrough of historical consciousness. Much of the tension and dramatic development in O'Connor's stories, I would argue, comes from the conflict between this Christian consciousness and the various forms of mythical, conventional, and historical consciousness also created in the stories.

It is tempting to equate this Christian consciousness in the stories with O'Connor herself and regard it as a manifestation of artistic persona. To do so is a mistake, I believe, because it misconstrues O'Connor's beliefs about the proper role of the artist and tends to reduce the reality present in the stories themselves. Robert Drake was perhaps closest to the truth when he observed that Jesus himself was the real hero in O'Connor's fiction. His remark suggests that the governing consciousness in the stories derives from O'Connor's witnessing to the source of mystery, personality, and free and creative action in history. O'Connor seemed to confirm this source of mystery when she noted that her stories themselves surprised her in the creation and that their implications often went beyond her powers of rational analysis. In short, what I think we see here is the mysterious action of grace within the creative act, creating the prophetic artist who stands in the long line of prophets whose acknowledged function is to reveal the true order of existence in history. As a writer, then, O'Connor witnessed to the essential mystery at the source of creative action, not merely in a general sense, but in the specific person of Christ. Thus all of her creative powers were concentrated on the creation of this prophetic consciousness. Symbol, character, and action all operate to create an encounter with mystery for the reader, an encounter with a world that is open-ended, full of possibility, and free.

When one examines the types of consciousness shown in O'Connor's characters, one discovers a considerable range in complexity, if we use the language of Voegelin and Thompson and understand complexity in terms of degrees of individuation or differentiation. This complexity is compounded by the dramatic situations through which major characters undergo radical change. Some experience breakthroughs to higher modes of consciousness and fuller self-discovery; some resist or reject these breakthroughs; some regress or attempt to regress to lower levels of consciousness. In the main, however, a process of complication of consciousness governs the major stories. Even those characters who reject the threatening possibility of a higher mode of existence paradoxically achieve a partial self-transcendence through loss. Even in rejection they gain a new consciousness, a new sense of identity, brought about by their violent displacement from a former mode of existence.

While it is impossible here to examine all of the specific forms and developments of consciousness in her fiction, several typical examples can be shown to represent the general pattern. Such examples, of course, cannot represent the full reality of the story, but they can serve to illustrate the wide range and complexity with which O'Connor was able to represent developing consciousness in her work, and I think help clarify the issues of her "primitivism" and her refusal to engage history.

Some of her characters, mostly minor figures, represent fixed modes of thought or reversions to simplistic levels of consciousness typical of the mythical or conventional levels. Enoch Emery in *Wise Blood* is a clear example of this type of character, with his rejection of reason, his indulgence in fantastic wish-fulfillment and worship of blood knowledge, and finally his comic degeneration into an "ape." Enoch wants only to find a friend and fit into the world and so allows himself to be governed completely by the world's conventions. Because he refuses truly human individuation or personality in the deepest sense, O'Connor classified him as a "moral moron." Other characters, though in less extreme degrees, represent similar examples of the mythical and/or conventional mind and remain essentially unchanged throughout their fictional lives: the prostitute Leora Watts and Mrs. Wally Bee Hitchcock in *Wise Blood,* Mrs. Crater in "The Life You Save May Be Your Own," Mr. and Mrs. Ashfield in "The River," and Mrs. Hopewell in "Good Country People."

A typical pattern in many stories, one treated in varying degrees of complexity, involves the radical change that occurs when a character possessed of a mythical or conventional mind is forced to encounter the possibilities and dangers inherent in the breakthrough to higher consciousness. Such is the case with Mrs. Cope in "A Circle In The Fire," Mrs. Shortley and Mrs. McIntyre in "The Displaced Person" (though with different results), the Grandmother in "A Good Man Is Hard To Find," and Mrs. May in "Greenleaf." Mrs. Cope and Mrs. Shortley suffer through violence to obtain a new self-understanding, a higher rational differentiation of *who they really are.* In both cases this greater self-knowledge and individuation involves a new perception of their place in history. At the crucial moment of breakthrough in both stories these women experience a personal identification with the suffering masses of European war victims, an image of a larger historical community of mystery and suffering which both women tended to deny earlier in favor of their self-enclosed mental worlds. But now this world is "opened," fraught with possibility, and both women become ruefully aware of their own engagement with this history. Paradoxically, both achieve self-transcendence through their fall, finding differentiation through symbolic union with Europe. And this larger order of reality, of mystery, which the women come to know through the action is made concrete by the governing Christian consciousness that O'Connor infuses into the stories. Mrs. Shortley and Mrs. Cope do not achieve that highest form of breakthrough in which the person explicitly experiences, as Voegelin claims, a divine revelation as the source of personality. The ultimate source is only implied here. As we shall see, O'Connor made the divine revelation explicit in very few stories. Nevertheless, Mrs. Shortley and Mrs. Cope do experience the divine revelation implicitly in the sense that they encounter mystery; most important, in the revelation the former situation of closure based on a false understanding of their place in the order of being is forever destroyed.

The Grandmother in "A Good Man Is Hard To Find" undergoes a similar kind of breakthrough to higher consciousness. In the Misfit's speeches about the pivotal significance of Jesus' Incarnation and Resurrection to history O'Connor came closer to an explicit statement of the Christian stance. Throughout most of the story the Grandmother exists closed off from reality, shut up within a conventional identity of herself as a southern lady. But in her encounter with the Misfit, she is slowly divested of this false persona and comes to recognize her bond—her analogical identity—with fallen humanity and her true place in history. Consequently, her gesture of touching the Misfit just before he kills her represents not only her breakthrough to a higher mode of consciousness but also an exercise of that creative freedom, that acknowledgment of self-responsibility ("Why you're one of my own babies!"), which is so characteristic of the breakthrough. As the Misfit tacitly recognizes, the Grandmother has found a truer source of personality in death: "She would of been a good woman . . . if it had been somebody there to shoot her every minute of her life."

Some characters are led to the possibility of breakthrough to more complex consciousness only to reject it; these characters prefer retrenchment or reversion instead. Such is the case with old Mr. Fortune in "A View of the Woods." At the end of this story, as we saw in chapter 4, Mr. Fortune ruthlessly rejects the view represented by the Pitts family and dies trying to escape its vital symbol—the trees. Mr. Fortune refuses any possibility of conversion. By contrast, a similar possibility of conversion is still open to the Misfit in "A Good Man Is Hard To Find," for even though he explicitly rejects "Jesus' he'p," his alternative ethic of "meanness" has clearly not satisfied him even after the murder of the Grandmother. The possibility is still open, as O'Connor noted in an essay, that he may "one day become the prophet he was meant to be."

The situation is more ambiguous in the case of Julian in "Everything That Rises Must Converge." Though the death of his mother precipitates a breakthrough in the sense that he now is forced to see that his identity has been based upon a parasitical dependence on her, in the end he seems desperately trying to retreat from history and the painful process of entering into a higher mode of consciousness. He cries "Help! Help!" after his mother dies, and as he runs, "the tide of darkness seemed to sweep him back to her, postponing from moment to moment his entry into the world of guilt and sorrow" (*Complete Stories,* p. 420). Perhaps Julian's reaction is only momentary, for as I have suggested he cannot really "go back" to his former mode of existence and thought. He may indeed advance along the lines of more authentic individuation, of rising to self-transcendence through convergence with history; or he may choose retrenchment into the kind of isolated, self-conscious closure of mind that has characterized so much of his thinking in the story. O'Connor keeps the tension of free choice vitally unresolved.

Much of O'Connor's creative energy was spent in dramatizing explicitly that type of historical consciousness characteristic of the modern mind since the Enlightenment. Many of her most important characters possess this self-awareness, most notably Hulga Hopewell, the Misfit, Sheppard, Asbury Fox before his final epiphany, and of course Rayber in *The Violent Bear It Away.* Each is in his own way a "self-created" individual, having "made" himself according to a rational model. Hulga has tried to forsake her identity as Joy in favor of a new identity as nihilist intellectual; she regards this self-conceived identity as her highest creative act. Similarly, the convict has named himself the Misfit in a radical act of self-conscious individuation.[11] Both characters possess an intense belief that reality is completely historically conditioned; they presume to have rationally penetrated history and critiqued it. "I call myself the Misfit," the convict says, "because I can't make what I done fit what all I gone through in punishment." And Hulga tells the Bible Salesman: "I have seen through to nothing." Thus Hulga's and the Misfit's acts of renaming represent human efforts at self-transcendence and freedom from the burdens of historical consciousness, but without reference to any source in a divine revelation. They have instead "created" and "called" themselves. Asbury Fox, as we saw, also tries to create himself anew as a modern artist, in reaction to his own past history. Even more explicitly, Rayber has attempted to remake himself according to his own rational model; he is ruthlessly driven to exclude any hint of mystery in being or possible transcendence. Rejecting the divine reality for a total embrace of secular humanism, he proclaims: "It's enough to be a man."

For each of these characters, mind itself has become the absolute measure of reality. Yet by following the idol of reason they become entrapped in alienation and closure, a situation dramatically revealed in two ways: by the larger order of reality made present within the story through narrative voice and by the irruption of mysterious forces that invade and disrupt their mind-conceived worlds. This irruption violently shatters their presumed identities to reveal both the limits of human reason and the delusive nature of their so-called intellectual "autonomy." Once prisoners of themselves, the characters are now at least freer to experience a larger possibility of being, a true open-endedness to the meaning of personality and history, whose source is ultimately mysterious. Closure is destroyed, at least in this particular action. In her defeat, Hulga must face the chastening new knowledge of the ignorance and false innocence she has shown in her encounter with Manley Pointer. Rayber must suffer the consequences of his ruthless rejection of the mystery of love after Bishop is drowned; Sheppard must suffer the failure of his humanistic dream for Johnson and Norton. For these historically self-conscious characters O'Connor creates a *via negativa* that ends in the ruin of their reason-founded selves and worlds. But in that ruin lies the possibility of a new and truer mode of consciousness that is no longer totally identified with reason, and the possibility of a truer personality, since at least in their moment of defeat they must experience *themselves* as mysteries, whether or not they finally choose to appropriate that wisdom.

Furthermore, when we look at O'Connor's stories for explicit examples of Christian consciousness within characters, as distinct from the Christian prophetic consciousness that governs the entire story, several come to mind. Some are minor characters and are revealed only externally; that is, O'Connor does not show the interior consciousness of these characters. Examples of this type of minor but important character include Mr. Guizac and the priest in "The Displaced Person," Father Finn in "The Enduring Chill," Mrs. Greenleaf in "Greenleaf," the nun in "A Temple of the Holy Ghost," and the preacher Bevel Summers in "The River." Old Tarwater, of course, is the most complex and extensive treatment of this explicit Christian consciousness; his consciousness is completely formed and manifested in its essence throughout the course of his existence in *The Violent Bear It Away.*

Several of her most important stories dramatize characters who experience a breakthrough to Christian consciousness; in this breakthrough their sense of the divine source of personality and of their true place in history is made explicit in a revelation. Although it is rendered implicitly, such is the case I think in *Wise Blood,* when the logic of Haze Motes's quest to transcend history first by innocence and then by nihilism is defeated and he is left to face his true fallen self. In his recognition that he is not "clean" we see the emergence of a new consciousness in which Haze acknowledges his need for repentance, that he must pay. In "The Artificial Nigger," O'Connor explicitly named the divine source of Mr. Head's personality, a breakthrough to higher consciousness in which he sees both himself and history as grounded in the Resurrection mode. Mr. Head's vision is a blinding epiphany of self-transcendence, of awakened self-responsibility, and of a true sense of identity:

> He stood appalled, judging himself with the thoroughness of God, while the action of mercy covered his pride like a flame and consumed it. He had never thought himself a great sinner before but he saw now that his true depravity had been hidden from him lest it cause him despair. He realized that he was forgiven for sins from the beginning of time, when he had conceived in his own heart the sin of Adam, until the present, when he had denied poor Nelson. He saw that no sin was too monstrous for him to claim as his own, and since God loved in proportion as He forgave, he felt ready at that instant to enter Paradise. (*Three by Flannery O'Connor*, pp. 213–14)

Similar epiphanies that show breakthroughs to modes of Christian consciousness occur in "The Enduring Chill" and "Revelation." For Asbury Fox, this breakthrough is linked explicitly to the Third Person of God, when "the last film of illusion was torn as if by a whirlwind from his eyes" and he sees "the Holy Ghost, emblazoned in ice instead of fire," descend upon him (*Complete Stories*, p. 382). In "Revelation" Ruby Turpin experiences the breakthrough in terms of a vision of the post-Final Resurrection when she sees herself among the "vast horde rumbling toward heaven." But this vision of her true self and her true place in salvation history comes only after the destruction of her former "mind," when she had reduced Christianity to a conventional mode of reality and presumed herself to be one of the "elect." Thus her final vision is a revelation of the mystery of history as well as its transcendent source.

The process of the complexification of consciousness, implicitly based on a Christocentric model, is dramatized in all of her major stories, yet O'Connor gave this process its fullest treatment in *The Violent Bear It Away*. Characters in other major stories—Asbury Fox, Mr. Head, and Mrs. Turpin for example—do experience the breakthrough to Christian consciousness, but in these cases the breakthrough is often dramatized obliquely or telescoped into a violent epiphanic moment of revelation. This oblique treatment may well be why her characters seem "primitive": they seem to move from one level of consciousness to another abruptly by some act of violent displacement, a kind of dramatic foreshortening that schematizes their development. Given the nature of theophanic irruption, this kind of foreshortening is both theologically valid, and a legitimate fictional practice within the limits of the short story. Nevertheless, such foreshortening may well inspire criticism of O'Connor's characters as being "simple," particularly since she placed such extreme demands upon her art by trying to capture the dynamic relationship of individual consciousness, the external world, and the transcendant, invisible order. Such criticism still seems to me to overlook the Christian prophetic consciousness which is present throughout the entire story, and this *total* order of reality, as I have argued, must finally be measured. Even allowing for this oversight, a further criticism might be registered: although many of her characters experience a breakthrough to higher consciousness which is implicitly or explicitly Christocentric, O'Connor does not show enough of that drama wherein different modes or levels of consciousness are shown to exist *simultaneously* within a single mind, "contending," as it were, as the process of development unfolds. This mental drama, the criticism might run, would be a truer representation of the complex consciousness in history, something equivalent to Warren's Jack Burden, Faulkner's Quentin Compson, or Welty's Virgie Rainey. As I have indicated, I do not believe such a criticism can be sustained if the *total* order of reality created in the short stories is examined. Nevertheless, full development of a complex consciousness from an internal perspective was something O'Connor seemed to be working toward in her career and which she achieved in *The Violent Bear It Away*. In the story of young Tarwater, O'Connor created her fullest and most mature dramatization of the development of Christian consciousness and personality in relation to history. Moreover, Tarwater's achievement of *simultaneous* levels of consciousness is rooted in an analogical view of reality; his mind, in effect, becomes in both form and content an analogical power or instrument. [12] In *The Violent Bear It Away*, I would argue, O'Connor achieved the fullest development of her analogical vision and the most complete identification of thought and technique. It is not surprising that the novel, viewed reflexively, is about the vocation of the word, the prophetic artist's call.

In creating young Tarwater O'Connor set out to dramatize the struggle toward full personal individuation along the lines of breakthrough of Christian and historical consciousness. This struggle is represented specifically by Tarwater's battle over his vocation and is cast precisely in terms of the central insight of the breakthrough in Hebrew axial consciousness: the experience of a "call" issuing from the divine being. Like the Israelites of the axial period, young Tarwater is under great pressure to decide *who he is* in the face of this call. His vocation to be a prophet will define his place within and relationship to history; like the prophetic artist, his mission is to create and interpret history in the light of its transcendent purpose.

Tarwater's spiritual struggle centers on the various modes of consciousness—mythical/conventional, historical, Christian—which exist simultaneously in his mind as possible modes of being to which he must respond. One option open to him is to revert to the level of the primitive-mythical, to ignore the call to individuation, self-responsibility, and decision. He can stay at home in Powderhead after his great-uncle's death, drink moonshine and "mind his bidnis." This option is offered by the "inner voice" that befriends him after old Tarwater's death, a voice that offers a "reasonable," utterly mundane, and self-enclosed view of the world and human personality. "Take it easy," the inner voice advises Tarwater: "I wouldn't pay too much attention to my Redemption if I was you. Some people take everything too hard" (*Three by Flannery O'Connor*, p. 330). As Tarwater begins to drink whiskey, the inner voice counsels him to see himself not even as part of human society, but only as primitive man obliged only to fulfill his own natural needs. It is a compelling voice, which, ironically, Tarwater is not even able to silence by getting drunk; it haunts him throughout the novel in the voice of strangers—the salesman Meeks, the homosexual rapist—who constantly offer this regressive mode of existence to Tarwater.

Coexistent with this voice of primitivistic wish fulfillment in young Tarwater's consciousness is another mode of thought—the biblical "mind" infused in him by old Tarwater and the specific call of his mission to baptize the idiot Bishop. From childhood Tarwater has been instructed by the great-uncle in the Christian conception of history, the Christocentric basis of human personality, and the meaning of responsibility to God's call. "I saved you to be free, your own self!" old Tarwater tells him. "I brought you out here to raise you a Christian, and more than a Christian, a prophet! . . . and the burden of it will be on you." This mode of thought constantly contends with the primitive voice co-present in Tarwater's mind, particularly in the opening section of the novel when Tarwater struggles to decide whether or not to give his great-uncle a proper Christian burial.

Yet to accept the prophetic identity marked out for him by his great-uncle without question would be a mistake, for in terms of his development, such uncritical acceptance would countervail personal differentiation; it would mean that young Tarwater had simply reduced the Christian vision to a mode of convention to follow. He would be accepting Christianity as just another datum of history, without *personal* response. In several stories, as I have shown, O'Connor clearly criticized that kind of mind which had so absorbed the Christian viewpoint, so enclosed it within history, as to reduce it to a mode of tradition and convention and thereby render it completely mundane and impersonal. Young Tarwater's sense of the danger of such submission is evident in his frequent arguments with his great-uncle that the injunction to baptize Bishop may not in fact be *his* call. He intuits that blind submission to old Tarwater's commands may mean a truncating of his own personality; it would frustrate by oversimplification that process of complexification wherein Tarwater must absorb, hold in dynamic tension, and freely act upon reality in light of the various modes of thought that present themselves simultaneously as options in his mind. A *unique* call from the divine must come *to him*. Ironically, he expects this to be in the form of a miraculous sign, such as a burning bush or the sun stopped in the sky, but the particular call he receives is as unheroic as it is undeniably clear to him:

> Tarwater clenched his fists. He stood like one condemned, waiting at the spot of execution. Then the revelation came, silent, implacable, direct as a bullet. He did not look into the eyes of any fiery beast or see a burning bush. He only knew, with a certainty sunk in despair, that he was expected to baptize the child he saw and begin the life his great uncle had prepared him for. He knew that he was called to be a prophet and that the ways of his prophecy would not be remarkable. His black pupils, glassy and still, reflected depth on depth his own stricken image of himself, trudging into the distance in the bleeding stinking mad shadow of Jesus, until at last he received his reward, a broken fish, a multiplied loaf. The Lord out of dust had created him, had made him blood and nerve and mind, had made him to bleed and weep and think, and set him in a world of loss and fire all to baptize one idiot child that He need not have created in the first place and to cry out a gospel just as foolish. (*Three by Flannery O'Connor*, pp. 357–58)

A third mode of thought which young Tarwater absorbs in the dynamic process of his mental growth is that rational self-conscious humanism offered by his uncle Rayber. Rayber is O'Connor's version of that type of secular rationalist which emerged in the second axial breakthrough of the Enlightenment. Intensely self-conscious, he rejects the Christian vision of history and personality as an archaic and warped vision of being, one that in his view proffers escapism from the "reality" of the human condition. For Rayber "reality" means a totally enclosed mundane order; notions of transcendence are delusory. Within this mundane order, he argues, "it is enough to be a man." For Rayber man is therefore a self-defining and self-sufficient being who creates his own identity in history according to a rational model. Though as a child he too was infused by old Tarwater with the Christian vision, Rayber claims to have ruthlessly exorcized that influence. He insists that young Tarwater must do likewise if he wants to become a man, fully autonomous and free. At the same time, Rayber denies any mystery that cannot be rationally penetrated by the human mind. Mind has become his god; all his psychic efforts are directed toward rational control of reality. In him personality and consciousness have become totally identified with mind.

Most significantly, what Rayber fears and cannot control by reason is the irrational love he felt for old Tarwater and continues to feel for the idiot Bishop. His love is a force of mystery, confounding all logic, which Rayber rigidly tries to control, but at the cost, ironically, of his very humanity, since his rejection of mysterious love is a denial of the source of being itself.

Young Tarwater intuits the spiritual impotence and inherent closure in Rayber's position, although he is partially attracted to Rayber's brand of humanism as a possible means of escape from the mysterious burden of religious consciousness infused by his great-uncle. In Rayber young Tarwater witnesses the loss of metaphysical freedom. He *knows* that Rayber can't act in any meaningful sense because he "lives in his head." Conversely, Tarwater proclaims that he can himself take action either in denial or affirmation of his prophetic mission. However, a mark of his pride is that he conceives of this freedom rationalistically and takes it as evidence of his own spiritual self-sufficiency. Only in the drowning of Bishop, when Tarwater inadvertently says the words of baptism, is he immersed in the full mystery of freedom.

O'Connor has created in Tarwater a dramatic portrait of a self-conscious mind that has absorbed contending visions of being, history, and personality, a mind which openly holds these visions in a state of creative tension as possibilities to be enacted in the encounter with reality, a mind developing in such a way that it will paradoxically come to know only through defeat the very limits of mind as a measure of reality. And finally, O'Connor created in Tarwater a mind that will finally locate and accept the transcendent, mysterious source of both personality and the meaning of a personhood in history. Thus the "action" of consciousness in young Tarwater, which is dramatized analogically as the novel unfolds, is characterized by openness and increasing complexity; the action is a process in which he moves dynamically toward a greater degree of individuation as he grows toward acceptance of his prophetic vocation.

In the final scene in the novel, Tarwater enters fully into an axial consciousness transformed by Christ's Resurrection, and O'Connor infuses the scene with all of the characteristics inherent in the Christocentric mind. Tarwater's drowning of Bishop was an attempt, conceived by self-sufficient reason, to destroy once and for all the burden of prophetic consciousness his great-uncle developed in him as a child, but his intention is inexplicably confounded when he utters the words of baptism over Bishop. Instead of simplifying his mental world by violently exorcizing the religious imperative, he now confronts an interior world of mystery which reason is powerless to control or comprehend fully. Tarwater still tries to escape by returning to Powderhead and denying his prophetic call, but the assault by the pervert mysteriously brings him a personal awareness of the radically evil denial of being and personhood which he committed in drowning Bishop and which he now has suffered at the hands of the pervert. Paradoxically, this shocking violation of his being leads Tarwater to accept his vocation.

Tarwater's newly-won discovery of the roots of his being and his commitment to the prophetic vocation are grounded in the vision of resurrection that William Thompson sees as the mark of specific Christian consciousness. At Powderhead, Tarwater receives a vision of the resurrected souls, including his great-uncle, being fed the Bread of Life in the form of loaves and fishes. Such a divine revelation, as Thompson and Voegelin argue, creates an eminently reasonable vision of the order of reality. The revelation enhances human reason by revealing its divine source as its proper object, beyond mutability and the power of death. In so doing, it both relativizes death and shatters that egocentric identification of reason with the whole of consciousness which plagued and defeated Rayber. In Tarwater, on the other hand, self-sufficient reason is defeated and replaced by a consciousness open to mystery. This resurrection vision thus enables him to act creatively in history and become "the man for others." Yet the resurrection vision is balanced by his commitment to enter the world, to go to the city, and to *"warn the children of God of the terrible speed of God's mercy" (Three by Flannery O'Connor,* p. 447). By his commitment Tarwater avoids the threat of gnostic dualism inherent in a perception of the transcendent order; he does not flee the world, and as O'Connor noted, his ministry will involve the way of crucifixion—suffering, defeat, and death.[13] His decision to "enter the world" is based on the perception that there are not two worlds, transcendent and immanent, but only one, the world that God created and that man co-creates by his actions. Such a decision implies that Tarwater has achieved, integrated, and transformed the historical consciousness of the second axial breakthrough, for his commitment to his vocation witnesses to his understanding of man's responsibility for his own salvation history.

Finally, while O'Connor makes clear that Tarwater has achieved a Christian consciousness at the end of the novel, this condition is neither static nor univocal. As Voegelin insists, other levels of awareness (mythical, conventional, historical) are still present in the complexified consciousness and still capable of being actuated; "regression" is always a possibility. Since what characterizes Tarwater's mind at the end is openness, possibility, and a sense of the mystery of being, there is nothing to preclude relapse or error, as indeed his great-uncle discovered when he mistakenly tried to enact his prophetic role without a clear "call." Tarwater will struggle with existence in the metaxy, Voegelin's "In-Between"; he will struggle with the dynamic mystery of being as he undergoes the process of discovering and creating the meaning of the Person in history. In Tarwater O'Connor created a complex and dramatic vision of the mind's engagement with history in all its ultimate extensions of meaning.

Conclusion

Except for the work being done in specialized academic disciplines, ours is not an age given to much concern with metaphysical speculations. Nevertheless, metaphysical notions are at the heart of one's vision and understanding of the dimensions of reality; any vision of reality presupposes a certain metaphysics. Yet as Brian Wicker has shown, the concept of the analogy of being has suffered particular neglect in our times; since the Enlightenment it has tended to be either ignored or discredited in favor of the associationist concepts of being espoused by Hume, Locke, Hartley, and others.[1] There is a fundamental incompatibility between these associationist views and the analogical view: the analogical view is based upon a *causal* relationship between existent things and between the terms of the analogy, and "causality involves the notion that all things in the world have natural tendencies to behave in *certain determinate and intelligible ways.*"[2] The analogical view of reality, then, affirms that an *order* exists in creation, not chaos or randomness, and that this order has its ultimate source in the divine creator. Such is also the view of Etienne Gilson when he argues that all creation is an analogue of God, the effect of the divine creative act.[3]

I have argued throughout this study that the metaphysics based upon an analogical view of reality is at the core of Flannery O'Connor's fictional vision and practice. I have also maintained that her vision and practice are rooted specifically in the historical Christ event, the Incarnation and Resurrection of Jesus. A few more words need to be said about the relation of this metaphysics and the Christ event to a concept which is rarely given much discussion when O'Connor's fiction is talked about—love.

All readers of O'Connor's fiction are quick to recognize that sin and man's fallen condition are of central concern in her stories. At the same time, she insisted on her belief in Christ's Redemption and in the *work* of that process of Redemption in history. Her well-known statement of belief has become so familiar that it threatens to lull us into neglecting to consider its profound implications: "I see from the standpoint of Christian orthodoxy. This means that for me the meaning of life is centered in our Redemption by Christ and what I see in the world I see in its relation to that."[4] This statement is, of course, a statement about analogy, and it leads logically to a consideration of this question: what does this belief, coupled with a recognition of man's sinful condition, have to do with the metaphysics of analogy, with love, and finally, with O'Connor as a comic writer?

The metaphysics of analogy affirms a fundamental order in creation, an order which has been diminished, though not destroyed, by human sin. The effect of sin was to put the powers of natural destruction and cosmic disintegration—what scripture terms the powers of sin and death—in the ascendancy, with dominion over creation. In such a situation only a law of "natural justice" can prevail, the kind of justice demanded by the Misfit. The Christ event is an act which destroys this law, defeats the evil powers and principalities, and reaffirms the fundamental order of creation. Redemption, therefore, is an act of creative power—the power of Christ's love. As Wicker says, Christ constitutes in his own person "resistance to the chaos and disintegration of the world. . . . The Christ of the gospels like the heroes or anti-heroes of many modern novels, is the arch-enemy of the cosmic collapse: the center of a life-asserting organization and energy directed towards the defeat of an otherwise inexorable process of disintegration."[5] To state the matter differently, we can say that Christ's Incarnation and Resurrection is the quintessential analogical action, one which recapitulates the original creative action of divine love by affirming the creative power of the spirit and reaffirming the fundamental goodness of creation. We can also say, I believe, that the Christ event is the quintessential comic reversal. If as Lynch maintains the comic action involves a return to the fundamental reality of our condition, then I believe the Christ event can be seen as an act of creative love united with the source of cosmic order.

It is in this sense that it seems to me proper to speak of Flannery O'Connor as a comic writer whose work is grounded in love. Her best stories analogically recapitulate the redemptive act by recalling the audience to the fundamental source of being. This recalling is achieved by comic reversal in the sense I have defined it, a reversal that involves suffering often to the point of death—the terrible *cost* of a "return to reality," to use O'Connor's own words. Yet the cost should not be confused with the reality; O'Connor constantly warns her audience to concentrate on the *meaning* of actions and not just to count the number of bodies by the side of the road. The central meaning underlying this comic reversal, I would maintain, is the creative power of divine love that in spite of everything man has lost through evil nevertheless validates the ultimate good of man and creation. It is no coincidence that in delineating Rayber's spiritual problem in *The Violent Bear It Away* O'Connor linked metaphysics to the ontology of love: Rayber can find no ultimate meaning in the universe because to him the mystery of love is "irrational" and "makes no sense." For O'Connor, the mystery of Christ's creative love is the foundation stone of the meaning of action in history. Thus she would concur, I believe, with Brian Wicker's observation: "For love is not the answer to the question *how* the world goes round, but *why* it exists at all."[6]

Notes

Introduction

1. *The Collected Works of St. John of the Cross*, trans. Kieran Kavanaugh, O.C.D., and Otilio Rodriquez, O.C.D. (Washington, D.C.: ICS Publications, 1979), p. 39.

2. Either explicit or implicit arguments for a strong Manichean strain in O'Connor's work can be found most conspicuously in John Hawkes' "Flannery O'Connor's Devil," *Sewanee Review* 70 (Summer 1962): 395–407, Martha Stephens' *The Question of Flannery O'Connor* (Baton Rouge: Louisiana State University Press, 1973), and Frederick Asals' *Flannery O'Connor: The Imagination of Extremity* (Athens: University of Georgia Press, 1982).

Chapter One

1. Throughout this discussion I have relied heavily but not exclusively on theologian Claude Tresmontant's *A Study of Hebrew Thought*. Tresmontant's book is a blueprint or "sketch of the organic structure of a metaphysics truly but implicitly contained in the Bible." Thus while not a work in biblical textual or linguistic criticism, it focuses upon a certain way of seeing reality which Tresmontant finds unique in the biblical texts as a whole. He distinguishes this way of seeing by comparison with Platonic and neo-Platonic perspectives, as well as those of Bergson and Plotinus. His work summarizes a traditional viewpoint which is compatible with many other Catholic theologians' views and, more important, compatible with the magisterium of Catholic doctrine to which O'Connor gave her allegiance.

Obviously there are many other approaches to the biblical texts in the ongoing process of exegesis, but Tresmontant's study is particularly useful here because of its emphasis on metaphysical themes. Moreover, O'Connor seems to have been quite familiar with his book; see Arthur F. Kinney, ed., *Flannery O'Connor's Library: Resources of Being*, p. 22. This is not of course to imply that her familiarity with Tresmontant's book is ipso facto justification for inclusion; nor is it to imply that the study provides any reductive ideological "solution" to her fiction. It does offer, I believe, a way of establishing a relationship among the metaphysical foundations of her work, her theological views, and her vision of history.

2. In his excellent study of the relationship between metaphysics and fiction, Brian Wicker makes a similar argument for the interrelationship of world view, metaphysics, and artistic practice; see *The Story-Shaped World*, esp. pp. 23–30.

Wicker sees the principle of analogy as the ground of this interrelationship, as I shall also argue later.

3. See Romans 12:2 and Ephesians 4:23.

4. Tresmontant, *A Study of Hebrew Thought*, p. 138.

5. In his seminal work *The Analogical Imagination*, theologian David Tracy argues along similar lines for seeing the Christ event as the core of "focal meaning" for the analogical imagination; see esp. pp. 423–29.

6. Anyone familiar with William F. Lynch's *Christ and Apollo* will recognize the extent of my debt to his study of the metaphysics of the literary imagination; see esp. his chapters 5–8.

7. For an excellent summary of Voegelin's idea, see Gerhardt Niemeyer's "Eric Voegelin's Philosophy and the Drama of Mankind."

8. Wicker, *Story-Shaped World*, pp. 7–8.

9. Ibid., p. 22; chapters 1–4 of his work give an excellent theoretical foundation for this claim.

10. Tracy, *Analogical Imagination*, pp. 413–14.

11. Ibid., pp. 438–41.

12. Lynch, *Christ and Apollo*, pp. 150–51; see also Wicker, *Story-Shaped World*, pp. 16–22.

13. Lynch, *Christ and Apollo*, p. 153 (my italics).

14. Some readers may feel that the quoted passage does not represent the total dramatic achievement of *A Fable*. I would argue, to the contrary, that the problem of "dissociation" of rhetoric from concrete action is at the heart of the major weaknesses in the novel.

15. Lynch, *Christ and Apollo*, p. 152.

16. Tresmontant, *Essai sur la pensee biblique*, quoted in Lynch, *Christ and Apollo*, p. 211.

17. Ibid., p. 188. According to Tracy, "in Christian systematics, the primary focal meaning will be the event of Jesus Christ (usually mediated through particular forms and particular traditions). That focal meaning *as event* will prove the primary analogue for the interpretation of the whole of reality" (*Analogical Imagination*, p. 408); see also pp. 421–38 passim.

Chapter Two

1. O'Connor, *Mystery and Manners*, p. 72.

2. For an excellent discussion of this theme, see Lewis P. Simpson's *The Brazen Face of History*, chapter 12, "What Survivors Do."

3. Asals, *Imagination of Extremity*, p. 14.

4. See Joseph Frank's "Spatial Form in Modern Literature," *Sewanee Review* 53 (Spring/Summer/Autumn 1945).

5. See Irving Howe's "The Idea of the Modern," in his *The Idea of the Modern in Literature and the Arts*. Brian Wicker affirms the same interrelationship between metaphysical viewpoint and language in his critique of structuralism:

"I have suggested that there is an implicit (if unacknowledged) ideological undercurrent to the structuralist principles with which this essay has dealt. This comes out in the incompatibility of the causal theory that we have found in the analogical/metonymic/syntagmatic dimension with the prevailing associationist concepts that still tend to surround 'scientific' thought. Historically, such associationism and such concepts of 'science' can be traced to the Enlightenment; in England, to the period of Locke, Hartley and Hume. It is not surprising therefore that today it should be widely rejected as just part of an oppressive and outworn bourgeois ideology. For the fundamentally arbitrary and unintelligible character of associationist thinking lends itself very easily to the creation of a false ideology. Once the metaphysical idea of Nature, as an order which exists independently of human thought, has been rejected, it is perhaps inevitable that people should turn for their sense of intelligibility and meaning to what they can create for themselves, and to call this 'Nature'. A good deal of Romantic thinking can be traced in this way to associationist influences even when their results—say the extremer manifestations of Benthamism—are the object of explicit rejection. From such a 'Nature' formed by men in their own image, the overwhelming urge to manipulate both Nature and other men for the sake of a 'meaningful' existence easily follows. Man's 'grandiose aspirations', to use Robbe-Grillet's phrase, are soon satisfied once external reality, or Nature in the pre-Enlightenment sense, ceases to stand in our way" (*Story-Shaped World*, pp. 30–31).

6. It is "closed" because Mrs. McIntyre resists the possibility of a numinous dimension to reality.

7. It is crucial to remember, of course, that for O'Connor this divine presence in the Eucharist is a reality, and not just a symbolic representation. Her comment to friends about the Eucharist is well known: "If it's only a symbol, to hell with it."

8. Here is O'Connor's comic treatment of the problem of the artist. Shiftlet's revival of the "dead" car is a mock version of the maker's attempts to infuse matter with spirit. As an artist he resembles William Lynch's portrayal of the gnostic maker who seeks a transcendent vision by circumventing the concrete— the Apollonian artistic spirit described in *Christ and Apollo*.

Chapter Three

1. O'Connor, *Three by Flannery O'Connor*, p. 9.

2. See esp. in this regard Martha Stephens' *The Question of Flannery O'Connor*, pp. 49–82.

3. The same analogical question is contained in Mrs. Turpin's puzzlement in "Revelation" about how she can be a "warthog" and be saved at the same time, i.e., both within the natural order and yet transformed by Christ's Redemption.

4. Lynch, *Christ and Apollo*, p. 115. O'Connor's extensive comments on the grotesque, which implicitly parallel those of Lynch, can be found in "Some

Aspects of the Grotesque in Southern Fiction," *Mystery and Manners*, pp. 36–50.

5. O'Connor, *Three by Flannery O'Connor*, p. 24. The fact that Haze is found near death at an "abandoned construction site," of course, completes the meaning of this image and reinforces the symbolic significance of his final commitment.

6. O'Connor used the phrase "crypto-Catholic" to describe old Tarwater, but it applies equally to Haze at the end of *Wise Blood*—a believer who, lacking the established Church and its sacramental life, is forced to enact his spiritual destiny on his own.

Chapter Four

1. Robert Fitzgerald, introduction to O'Connor's *Everything That Rises Must Converge*.

2. See 1 Corinthians 6, 12:12–31, and 15.

3. In an early letter to "A," O'Connor comments on the Incarnation: "For you it may be a matter of not being able to accept what you call a suspension of the laws of the flesh and the physical, but for my part I think that when I know what the laws of the flesh and the physical really are, then I will know what God is. We know them as we see them, not as God sees them. For me it is the virgin birth, the Incarnation, the resurrection which are the true laws of the flesh and the physical. Death, decay, destruction are the suspension of these laws. I am always astonished at the emphasis the Church puts on the body. It is not the soul she says will rise but the body, glorified. . . . The resurrection of Christ seems the high point in the law of nature . . ." (The Habit of Being, p. 100).

4. Etienne Gilson, *The Spirit of Medieval Philosophy;* trans. chapter 5 contains an excellent discussion of analogy in relation to history.

5. See my essay "Flannery O'Connor, Henry James, and The International Theme," *Flannery O'Connor Bulletin* (1980).

6. Obviously the pattern is similar to that in "A Good Man Is Hard To Find." The Grandmother's confrontation with the Misfit leads her to recognize her true identity in history; but here, Julian's mother's confrontation leads her finally to turn away from that recognition.

7. See my essay "The Lessons of History: Flannery O'Connor's 'Everything That Rises Must Converge,'" pp. 39–45.

8. Perhaps the most fascinating aspect of Teilhard's evolutionary view of history, of course, if his notion of the convergence of consciousness into a "noosphere" as the apex of the process of "rising."

9. Mark 8:22–27.

10. O'Connor, *Mystery and Manners*, p. 184.

11. For an excellent discussion of this, see Walter Sullivan's essay "The New Faustus: The Southern Renascence and The Southern Aesthetic," in *Death by Melancholy*.

12. In "Parker's Back" particularly, we can see how far O'Connor had grown in her deepening of the theme of "the body" from the problematical and oblique treatment of it in the ending of *Wise Blood.*

Chapter Five

1. Percy, "Notes for a Novel About the End of the World," in *The Message in the Bottle*, p. 113.
2. Gilson, *The Spirit of Medieval Philosophy*, p. 138. The classic expression of this theme is found in chapter 10 of St. Augustine's *Confessions.*
3. Lynch, *Christ and Apollo*, pp. 110–15 passim; see my discussion of this in chapter 3.
4. McKenzie, *The Power and the Wisdom*, pp. 72–84 passim.

Chapter Six

1. The word "primitive" itself is, of course, open to various interpretations. Compared to some of Faulkner's characters, or in terms of actual social reality, O'Connor's characters may indeed seem to be "primitive." On the other hand, viewed in terms of their capacities for conscious experience, particularly experience of the numinous, her characters may not seem "primitive" at all.
2. Particularly helpful to this present study were the following: Jacques Maritain, *Creative Intuition in Art and Poetry;* Mircea Eliade, *The Sacred and the Profane;* Etienne Gilson, *The Spirit of Medieval Philosophy;* William F. Lynch, *Christ and Apollo;* William M. Thompson, *Christ and Consciousness;* and Gerhart Niemeyer, "Eric Voegelin's Philosophy and the Drama of Mankind." I owe a particular debt of gratitude to Niemeyer, Lynch, and Thompson for concepts developed in this chapter.
3. Thompson, *Christ and Consciousness*, pp. 19–44.
4. I am of course speaking of man in the generic sense. The "leap" in being" was made possible to man by the breakthrough; it does not mean that all or even many individuals actually achieved it.
5. Thompson prefers the term "sublational" to describe this view. Lynch describes this deepening of the possibilities of being in terms of the human imagination's acquiring and developing analogical, theological, and finally Christological potentialities; see *Christ and Apollo*, esp. chapter 8, "The Christian Imagination."
6. Gerhart Niemeyer, "Eric Voegelin's Philosophy and the Drama of Mankind," p. 33.
7. Thompson, *Christ and Consciousness*, pp. 61–74.
8. See *The Brazen Face of History*, chapters 11–13. Walker Percy offers similar observations in *The Message in the Bottle*, pp. 112–13.
9. Quoted in Thompson, *Christ and Consciousness*, p. 125.
10. Maritain, *Art and Scholasticism and the Frontiers of Poetry*, p. 28.

11. These rebellious acts of naming represent, of course, parodies of the creation of personality, with its divine source.

12. Conversely, Rayber's rationalistic reduction of reality is an attempted collapse of the mystery of analogy.

13. O'Connor, *The Habit of Being*, p. 359.

Conclusion

1. Wicker, *The Story-Shaped World*, pp. 30–32.

2. Ibid., pp. 20–22, 76–77, my italics.

3. Gilson, *The Spirit of Medieval Philosophy*, chapter 5, "Analogy, Causality, and Finality," pp. 84–108.

4. O'Connor, *Mystery and Manners*, p. 32.

5. Wicker, *Story-Shaped World*, p. 67.

6. Ibid.

Bibliography

Works marked with an asterisk indicate that they were part of O'Connor's personal library and are contained in the Flannery O'Connor Collection at Georgia College, Milledgeville.

Asals, Frederick. *Flannery O'Connor: The Imagination of Extremity*. Athens: University of Georgia Press, 1982.
______. "The Mythic Dimensions of Flannery O'Connor's 'Greenleaf'." *Studies in Short Fiction* 5 (Summer 1968): 317–30.
*Augustine. *The Confessions*. Translated by F. J. Sheed. New York: Sheed and Ward, 1943.
*Barth, Karl. *Evangelical Theology: An Introduction (Einfuhrung in die evangelische theologie)*. Translated by Grover Foley. New York: Holt, Rhinehart and Winston, 1963.
Baumbach, Jonathan. *The Landscape of Nightmare*. New York: New York University Press, 1965.
Browning, Preston M., Jr. *Flannery O'Connor*. Carbondale: Southern Illinois University Press, 1974.
*Buber, Martin. *Between Man and Man*. Translated by Ronald Gregor Smith. 1947. Reprint. Humanities Series. Boston: Beacon Press, 1955.
* ______. *Eclipse of God: Studies in the Relation Between Religion and Philosophy*. 1952. Reprint. New York: Harper and Brothers, Harper Torchbooks, 1957.
Burns, Stuart L. "The Evolution of *Wise Blood.*" *Modern Fiction Studies* 16 (1970): 147–62.
______. "Flannery O'Connor's *The Violent Bear It Away:* Apotheosis in Failure." *Sewanee Review* 76 (1968): 319–36.
*Caponigri, A. Robert, ed. *Modern Catholic Thinkers: An Anthology*. New York: Harper and Brothers, 1960.
*Corte, Nicholas. *Pierre Teilhard de Chardin: His Life and Spirit*. Translated by Martin Jarret-Kerr, C. R. 1957. Reprint. New York: Macmillan, 1960.
Cullman, Oscar. *Christ and Time*. Translated by Floyd V. Filson. Philadelphia: Westminster Press, 1950.
*D'Arcy, M. C., S. J. *The Meaning and Matter of History: A Christian View*. New York: Farrar, Straus and Cudahy, 1959.
* ______. *The Meeting of Love and Knowledge: Perennial Wisdom*. World Perspective Series, vol. 15. New York: Harper and Brothers, 1957.
* ______. *The Nature of Belief*. 1931. Reprint. St. Louis: B. Herder, 1958.
*Dawson, Christopher. *The Dynamics of World History*. Edited by John J. Mulloy. 1956. Reprint. New York: New American Library, 1962.

Bibliography

Desmond, John F. "Flannery O'Connor's Sense of Place." *Southern Humanities Review* 10 (Summer 1976): 251–59.

————. "The Lessons of History: Flannery O'Connor's 'Everything That Rises Must Converge.'" *Flannery O'Connor Bulletin* (Fall 1972): 39–45.

————. "The Mystery of the Word and the Act: Flannery O'Connor's *The Violent Bear It Away*." *American Benedictine Review* (1971): 342–47.

Drake, Robert. *Flannery O'Connor: A Critical Essay*. Grand Rapids: William B. Eerdmans, 1966.

Driskell, Leon V., and Joan T. Brittain. *The Eternal Crossroads: The Art of Flannery O'Connor*. Lexington: University of Kentucky Press, 1971.

Dunne, John S. *A Search for God in Time and Memory*. Notre Dame, Ind.: University of Notre Dame Press, 1977.

Eggenschwiler, David. *The Christian Humanism of Flannery O'Connor*. Detroit: Wayne State University Press, 1972.

Eliade, Mircea. *Cosmos and History: The Myth of the Eternal Return*. New York: Harper and Row, Harper Torchbooks, 1959.

————. *Myth and Reality*. New York: Harper and Row, Harper Torchbooks, 1963.

*————. *Patterns in Comparative Religions*. New York: Meridian Books, 1966.

————. *The Sacred and the Profane*. New York: Harcourt, Brace and World, 1959.

Faulkner, William. *A Fable*. New York: Random House, 1950.

Feeley, Sister Kathleen. *Flannery O'Connor: Voice of the Peacock*. New Brunswick, N.J.: Rutgers University Press, 1972.

Frank, Joseph. "Spatial Form in Modern Literature." *Sewanee Review* 53 (Spring/Summer/Autumn 1945): 221–40, 433–56, 643–53.

Friedman, Melvin J., and Lewis A. Lawson, eds. *The Added Dimension: The Art and Mind of Flannery O'Connor*. New York: Fordham University Press, 1966.

Getz, Lorine M. *Flannery O'Connor: Her Life, Library, and Book Reviews*. New York: Edwin Mellen Press, 1980.

Gilson, Etienne. *The Philosophy of St. Thomas Aquinas*. St. Louis: B. Herder Co., 1937.

————. *The Spirit of Medieval Philosophy*. New York: Charles Scribner's Sons, 1936.

*————. *The Unity of Philosophical Experience*. New York: Charles Scribner's Sons, 1937.

Goldbrunner, Josef. *Holiness is Wholeness*. Translated by Stanley Goodman. New York: Pantheon, 1955.

Gordon, Caroline. "Flannery O'Connor's *Wise Blood*." *Critique* 2 (1958): 3–10.

*Guardini, Romano. *The Conversion of Augustine*. Westminster, Md.: Newman Press, 1960.

————. *The End of the Modern World*. New York: Sheed and Ward, 1956.

*————. *Freedom, Grace, and Destiny: Three Chapters in the Interpretation of Existence*. New York: Pantheon, 1961.

*————. *The Lord*. Chicago: Henry Regnery, 1954.

*————. *Meditations Before Mass*. Westminster, Md.: Newman Press, 1956.

*Guitton, Jean. *The Modernity of St. Augustine*. Baltimore: Helicon Press, 1959.

Gunn, Giles. *The Interpretation of Otherness*. New York: Oxford University Press, 1979.

Hawkes, John. "Flannery O'Connor's Devil." *Sewanee Review* 70 (Summer 1962): 395–407.

Hendin, Josephine. *The World of Flannery O'Connor*. Bloomington: Indiana University Press, 1970.

Howe, Irving. *The Idea of the Modern in Literature and the Arts*. New York: Horizon, 1977.

Hyman, Stanley Edgar. *Flannery O'Connor*. Minneapolis: University of Minnesota Press, 1966.

*James, William. *The Varieties of Religious Experience: A Study in Human Nature*. New York: Crowell-Collier, 1961.

*Jarret-Kerr, Martin, C. R. *Studies in Literature and Belief*. London: Rockliff, 1954.

*John of the Cross, St. Bruno, Father, O.D.C. *St. John of the Cross*. New York: Sheed and Ward, 1932.

*Jung, Karl. *Modern Man in Search of a Soul*. 1933. Reprint. New York: Harcourt, Brace, 1957.

Kinney, Arthur F. *Flannery O'Connor's Library: Resources of Being*. Athens: University of Georgia Press, 1985.

*Lawler, Justus George. *The Christian Imagination: Studies in Religious Thought*. Westminster, Md.: Newman Press, 1955.

Lawson, Lewis A. "Flannery O'Connor and the Grotesque: *Wise Blood*." *Renascence* 17 (1965): 137–47, 156.

*Lewis, C. S. *The Problem of Pain*. 1940. Reprint. New York: Macmillan, 1962.

Lynch, William F. *Christ and Apollo: The Dimensions of the Literary Imagination*. New York: Sheed and Ward, 1960.

*————. *The Integrating Mind: An Exploration into Western Thought*. New York: Sheed and Ward, 1962.

*Malevez, L., S.J. *The Christian Message and Myth: The Theology of Rudolph Bultmann*. Westminster, Md.: Newman Press, 1958.

*Maritain, Jacques. *Art and Scholasticism and The Frontiers of Poetry*. New York: Charles Scribner's Sons, 1937.

*————. *Creative Intuition in Art and Poetry*. Cleveland: World Publishing Co., 1953.

————. *The Dream of Descartes*. Translated by Mabel F. Andison. New York: Philosophical Library, 1944.

*————. *A Preface to Metaphysics: Seven Lectures on Being*. New York: New American Library, 1962.

*————. *The Range of Reason*. New York: Charles Scribner's Sons, 1952.

Martin, Carter. *The True Country: Themes in the Fiction of Flannery O'Connor*. Nashville: Vanderbilt University Press, 1969.

Bibliography

May, John R. *The Pruning Word: The Parables of Flannery O'Connor.* Nashville: Vanderbilt University Press, 1969.

———. *Towards a New Earth: Apocalypse in the American Novel.* Notre Dame, Ind.: University of Notre Dame Press, 1972.

McKenzie, John L. *The Power and the Wisdom: An Interpretation of the New Testament.* New York: Doubleday, Image Books, 1972.

*———. *The Two-Edged Sword: An Interpretation of the Old Testament.* New York: Doubleday, Image Books, 1966.

McKnight, Stephen A., ed. *Eric Voegelin's Search for Order in History.* Baton Rouge: Louisiana State University Press, 1978.

Milder, Robert. "The Protestantism of Flannery O'Connor." *Southern Review* 11 (1975): 802–19.

Montgomery, Marion. "A Sense of Violation: Notes Toward a Definition of Southern Fiction." *Georgia Review* 19 (1965): 278–87.

———. *Why Flannery O'Connor Stayed Home.* Vol. 1 of *The Prophetic Poet and the Spirit of the Age.* LaSalle, Ill.: Sherwood Sugden and Co., 1981.

*Mounier, Emmanual. *The Character of Man.* Translated by Cynthia Rowland. New York: Harper and Brothers, 1956.

*———. *Personalism.* Translated by Philip Mairet. New York: Grove Press, 1952.

Muller, Gilbert H. *Nightmares and Visions: Flannery O'Connor and the Catholic Grotesque.* Athens: University of Georgia Press, 1972.

*Newman, John Henry Cardinal. *Apologia Pro Vita Sua.* New York: Modern Library, 1950.

Niemeyer, Gerhardt. "Eric Voegelin's Philosophy and the Drama of Mankind." *Modern Age* 20 (1976): 28–39.

O'Connor, Flannery. *The Complete Stories of Flannery O'Connor.* New York: Farrar, Straus and Giroux, 1971.

———. *Everything That Rises Must Converge.* Introduction by Robert Fitzgerald. New York: Farrar, Straus and Giroux, 1965.

———. *The Habit of Being.* Edited by Sally Fitzgerald. New York: Farrar, Straus and Giroux, 1979.

———. *Mystery and Manners.* Edited by Sally and Robert Fitzgerald. New York: Farrar, Straus and Giroux, 1969.

———. *The Presence of Grace and Other Book Reviews.* Compiled by Leo J. Zuber. Edited by Carter W. Martin. Athens: University of Georgia Press, 1983.

———. *Three by Flannery O'Connor.* New York: New American Library, 1964.

Orvell, Miles. *Invisible Parade: The Fiction of Flannery O'Connor.* Philadelphia: Temple University Press, 1972.

*Peguy, Charles. *Temporal and Eternal.* 1955. Reprint. New York: Harper and Brothers, 1958.

Percy, Walker. *The Message in the Bottle.* New York: Farrar, Straus and Giroux, 1976.

Phelan, Gerald B. *St. Thomas and Analogy.* Milwaukee: Marquette University Press, 1948.

*Pieper, Josef. *Belief and Faith: A Philosophical Tract.* New York: Pantheon, 1963.

*Poulet, Georges. *Studies in Human Time.* Translated by Elliott Coleman. New York: Harper and Brothers, Harper Torchbooks, 1959.

*Rabut, Olivier, O.P. *Teilhard de Chardin: A Critical Study.* New York: Sheed and Ward, 1961.

Scott, Nathan, ed. *Adversity and Grace.* Chicago: University of Chicago Press, 1968.

Simpson, Lewis P. *The Brazen Face of History: Studies in the Literary Consciousness of America.* Baton Rouge: Louisiana State University Press, 1980.

——. *The Dispossessed Garden: Pastoral and History in Southern Literature.* Athens: University of Georgia Press, 1975.

——. *The Man of Letters in New England and the South.* Baton Rouge: Louisiana State University Press, 1973.

Stephens, Martha. *The Question of Flannery O'Connor.* Baton Rouge: Louisiana State University Press, 1973.

Sullivan, Walter. *Death by Melancholy: Essays on Modern Southern Fiction.* Baton Rouge: Louisiana State University Press, 1972.

——. *A Requiem for the Renascence.* Athens: University of Georgia Press, 1976.

Tate, James O. "Faith and Fiction: Flannery O'Connor and the Problem of Belief." *Flannery O'Connor Bulletin* 5 (1976): 105–11.

*Tavard, George H., A.A. *Transiency and Permanence: The Nature of Theology According to St. Bonaventure.* St. Bonaventure, N.Y.: Franciscan Institute, 1954.

*Teilhard de Chardin, Pierre. *The Divine Milieu: An Essay on the Interior Life.* New York: Harper and Brothers, 1960.

*——. *The Phenomenon of Man.* New York: Harper and Brothers, 1959.

*Thomas Aquinas, Saint. *Introduction to Saint Thomas Aquinas.* Edited by Anton Pegis. New York: Modern Library, 1948.

Thompson, William M. *Christ and Consciousness.* New York: Paulist Press, 1977.

Tracy, David. *The Analogical Imagination: Christian Theology and the Culture of Pluralism.* New York: Crossroads, 1981.

*Tresmontant, Claude. *A Study of Hebrew Thought.* Translated by Michael Francis Gibson. New York: Desclee Company, 1960.

*Vawter, Bruce. *The Conscience of Israel: Pre-exilic Prophets and Prophecy.* New York: Sheed and Ward, 1961.

*Voegelin, Eric. *Israel and Revelation.* Vol. 1 of *Order and History.* Baton Rouge: Louisiana State University Press, 1956.

*——. *The World of the Polis.* Vol. 2 of *Order and History.* Baton Rouge: Louisiana State University Press, 1957.

*——. *Plato and Aristotle.* Vol. 3 of *Order and History.* Baton Rouge: Louisiana State University Press, 1957.

*von Hugel, Baron Friedrick. *Essays and Addresses on the Philosophy of Religion: First Series.* New York: E. P. Dutton, 1949.

Bibliography

*———. *Essays and Addresses on the Philosophy of Religion: Second Series*. New York: E. P. Dutton, 1951.

*———. *Letters from Baron von Hugel to a Niece*. Chicago: Henry Regnery Co., 1955.

Walters, Dorothy. *Flannery O'Connor*. New York: Twayne, 1973.

*Weigel, Gustave, S.J. *The Modern God: Faith in a Secular Culture*. New York: Macmillan, 1963.

Westling, Louise. *Sacred Groves and Ravaged Gardens: The Fiction of Eudora Welty, Carson McCullers, and Flannery O'Connor*. Athens: University of Georgia Press, 1985.

*White, Victor, O.P. *God and the Unconscious*. Chicago: Henry Regnery Co., 1953.

*———. *Soul and Psyche: An Inquiry into the Relationship of Psychotherapy and Religion*. New York: Harper and Brothers, 1960.

Wicker, Brian. *The Story-Shaped World: Fiction and Metaphysics: Some Variations on a Theme*. Notre Dame, Ind.: University of Notre Dame Press, 1975.

*Woods, Ralph L., ed. *The Catholic Companion to the Bible*. Philadelphia: J. B. Lippincott, 1956.

Index